52
Bible Drills and Quizzes

Easy-to-do Activities for Ages 6 -12

Publisher	*Arthur L. Miley*
Author	*Nancy S. Williamson*
Vice President	*Carolyn Passig Jensen*
Art Director	*Debbie Birch*
Cover Design	*Court Patton*
Production Director	*Barbara Bucher*
Illustrators	*Fran Kizer*
	Doug Ten Napel
Production Artist	*Andrew Smith*
Proofreaders	*Barbara Bucher*

Copyright © 1996 • Seventh Printing
Rainbow Books • P.O. Box 261129 • San Diego, CA 92196

#RB36168
ISBN 0-937282-66-9

Study to shew thyself approved unto God,

a workman that needeth not to be ashamed,

rightly dividing the word of truth.

2 Timothy 2:15

Search the scriptures; for . . . they . . . testify of Me.

John 5:39

Thy word have I hid in mine heart,

that I might not sin against Thee.

Psalm 119:11

52 Bible Drills and Quizzes

Easy-to-do Activities for Ages 6 -12

Introduction

Knowing how to study God's Word is one of the most important skills any Christian can have, yet Bible study is often neglected by many Christians because they have never learned how to effectively and enjoyably study the Bible.

This no longer needs to be true for your students.

This book contains 52 exciting Bible drills and quizzes which will get your children into God's Word, and help them study it, learn from it and enjoy it.

Numerous Bible quizzes in this book question the children about Bible people, places, events and other facts. Several quizzes and activities also help teach the books of the Bible. In addition, the Bible drills in this book develop the students' skills in quickly and accurately locating, reading, comprehending and responding to Scripture passages. Together the 52 Bible drills and quizzes, along with hundreds of quiz questions and Scripture passages, teach skills which are critical to studying and understanding God's Word; if a child can't understand what he is reading, he will have very little desire to continue to read or study the Bible.

The purpose of this book is three-fold:
1. To teach and review Bible facts and concepts through exciting activities of all kinds.
2. To teach children Bible-use skills and how to enjoy studying the Bible.
3. To help children discover what the Bible says to them and how it relates to their lives, by teaching them to find, read, understand and respond to Scriptures in exciting, competitive Bible drills and quizzes.

The 52 exciting drills and quizzes in this book are varied to provide exciting activities for every setting and every age. Many of the drills and quizzes are suitable for competitive quiz teams, either as formats to be used in competition or as a way to bring variety and new challenge to practice quizzing.

Activities of every sort are included: quiet quizzes, active drills and quizzes, "noisy" games ideal for outdoors, board games, independent study activities, and much more. Plus this book includes many unique "formats" for drills and quizzes, plus many thematic drills and quizzes, complete with questions, answers and/or Scripture references.

Most activities can be adapted for older or younger groups (or groups having less Bible knowledge) simply by substituting other quiz questions or Scriptures from those in this book. Unless marked otherwise, all Scriptures are from the King James Version, but any translation may be used effectively. Questions, activity sheets and other materials may be copied for classroom use.

These 52 Bible drills and quizzes are designed to be quick, easy and effective to use. You'll find something else — these drills and quizzes make it fun for your children to study and learn about the Bible too!

52 Bible Drills and Quizzes

Easy-to-do Activities for Ages 6 -12

CONTENTS

Bible Verse Drill

OBJECTIVE: Gets your students excited about finding Bible verses

Appropriate for ages 9 to 12 • For 4 or more students

Effective, exciting, enthusiastic Bible Verse Drills may be conducted using any Scripture references desired. You may choose verses which follow a definite theme, and/or are in keeping with the purpose of your lesson or unit of study. To get you started, the suggested Bible verses below include some of the "precious promises" of the Bible.

To conduct a drill, each child must have a Bible, holding it closed on either his lap or on the table or desk in front of him. Give the Bible reference followed by "Go." Immediately, the children begin to find the verse in the Bible. The first child to find the verse stands up and reads the verse aloud to the group, prefacing it with the correct reference. (If desired, all the children can read the verse together; in this manner the message of the verse will reach all the students.)

Score may be kept and the person who most often finds the verse first may be declared the winner. With some groups, however, this can have the effect of negatively motivating the students who consistently cannot find the Scriptures first. Evaluate your own class and do what works for you and your students.

Suggested Bible Verses:
John 15:7 — If ye abide in Me, and My words abide in you, ye shall ask what ye will, and it shall be done unto you.

Ephesians 6:11 — Put on the whole armour of God, that ye may be able to stand against the wiles of the devil.

Matthew 11:28 — Come unto Me, all ye that labour and are heavy laden, and I will give you rest.

Psalm 103:12 — As far as the east is from the west, so far hath He removed our transgressions from us.

Proverbs 18:10 — The name of the Lord is a strong tower: the righteous runneth into it, and is safe.

Titus 3:5 — Not by works of righteousness which we have done, but according to His mercy He saved us, by the washing of regeneration, and renewing of the Holy Ghost.

Revelation 21:7 — He that overcometh shall inherit all things; and I will be his God, and he shall be My son.

Philippians 1:6 — Being confident of this very thing, that He which hath begun a good work in you will perform it until the day of Jesus Christ.

John 3:17 — For God sent not His Son into the world to condemn the world; but that the world through Him might be saved.

Jeremiah 29:13 — And ye shall seek Me, and find Me, when ye shall search for Me with all your heart.

Hebrews 7:25 — Wherefore He is able also to save them to the uttermost that come unto God by Him, seeing He ever liveth to make intercession for them.

Jude 21 — Keep yourselves in the love of God, looking for the mercy of our Lord Jesus Christ unto eternal life.

Romans 8:14 — For as many as are led by the Spirit of God, they are the sons of God.

Isaiah 55:6 — Seek ye the LORD while He may be found, call ye upon Him while He is near.

Joshua 1:9 — Have not I commanded thee? Be strong and of a good courage; be not afraid, neither be thou dismayed: for the LORD thy God is with thee whithersoever thou goest.

Psalm 126:3 — The LORD hath done great things for us; whereof we are glad.

Lamentations 3:22 — It is of the LORD'S mercies that we are not consumed, because His compassions fail not.

2 Bible Reading Drill

OBJECTIVE: Creative way for students to learn locations of Scripture passages

Appropriate for ages 9 to 12 • For 4 or more students

Begin the drill with the students holding their Bibles. The teacher begins reading a Scripture passage. (If desired, students may be told the Bible book in which the passage is found.)

As soon as the teacher begins reading, the students may begin looking for the location of the passage in the Bible. The teacher continues reading until a student stands or raises his hand to indicate he has found the Scripture location.

Another idea:

When a student has found the passage, he stands. The teacher stops reading and the student begins reading. He reads until the next student finds the passage. After several students have found the passage, the teacher may start a new passage.

3 Bible Sit Down

OBJECTIVE: Reviews Bible facts or memory verses

Appropriate for ages 9 to 12 • For 8 or more students

Divide your class into two teams who stand facing one another. The teacher begins by asking the first team a Bible quiz question, Bible verse or reference. If a person on that team can correctly answer the question, or recite either the verse or the reference, he stays in the game. If he answers incorrectly, he must sit down and a member of the other team is given the opportunity to answer the question or recite the correct verse or reference. The teacher then asks the second team a new question or verse. The game continues until members of only one team are left standing.

Choose Bible quiz questions or Scriptures from those in this book, or from recent lessons.

4 Sword Drill

OBJECTIVE: Exciting ways to add military color to your Bible drills

Appropriate for ages 9 to 12 • For 4 or more students

This is a variation of the regular Bible Verse Drill, but with a little added military color, which greatly appeals to children—especially juniors. Show them that the Bible is the sword of the Spirit (Ephesians 6:17) and sharper than any two-edged sword (Hebrews 4:12). Then follow by giving this series of milliary commands:

"Attention!" (Students sit up or stand with closed Bibles in their hands.)

"Draw swords!" (Bibles are held high in right hands.)

"John 3:16." (The Bible reference is given.)

"John 3:16." (The students repeat the reference after the leader.)

"Charge!" (They begin searching for the verse.)

The first person to find the verse stands to his feet (or raises his hand). Score may be kept for the drill to determine who has found the most verses. Use the following Scripture verses or choose verses which follow a definite theme, and/or relate to your lesson or unit of study.

DRAW SWORDS

Suggested Bible Verses:

2 Peter 3:18 — But grow in grace, and in the knowledge of our Lord and Saviour Jesus Christ. To Him be glory both now and for ever. Amen.

John 6:63 — It is the spirit that quickeneth; the flesh profiteth nothing: the words that I speak unto you, they are spirit, and they are life.

Isaiah 45:22 — Look unto Me, and be ye saved, all the ends of the earth: for I am God, and there is none else.

Job 5:17 — Behold, happy is the man whom God correcteth: therefore despise not thou the chastening of the Almighty.

Exodus 20:7 — Thou shalt not take the name of the LORD thy God in vain; for the LORD will not hold him guiltless that taketh His name in vain.

Psalm 37:23 — The steps of a good man are ordered by the LORD: and He delighteth in his way.

Luke 23:43 — And Jesus said unto him, Verily I say unto thee, To day shalt thou be with Me in paradise.

Romans 12:1 — I beseech you therefore, brethren, by the mercies of God, that ye present your bodies a living sacrifice, holy, acceptable unto God, which is your reasonable service.

Matthew 9:38 — Pray ye therefore the LORD of the harvest, that He will send forth laborers into His harvest.

Joel 2:28 — And it shall come to pass afterward, that I will pour out My spirit upon all flesh; and your sons and your daughters shall prophesy, your old men shall dream dreams, your young men shall see visions.

Ephesians 4:30 — And grieve not the holy Spirit of God, whereby ye are sealed unto the day of redemption.

1 Timothy 2:5 — For there is one God, and one mediator between God and men, the man Christ Jesus.

Mark 10:27 — And Jesus looking upon them saith, With men it is impossible, but not with God: for with God all things are possible.

5 Bible Bowl

OBJECTIVE: Exciting format for competitive quizzing

Appropriate for age 9 to teens • For 4 to 8 students

This Bible review quiz is patterned after television's "College Bowl," and is both educational and interesting.

The equipment you need is a series of electric relays installed on four light bulb sockets so when one "contestant" pushes his button to answer a question none of the other lights can come on. Either two or four persons may make up a team.

Choose Bible quiz questions from recent lessons or units of study, or from the questions in this book.

Begin play by giving a "toss-up" question worth five points. The first contestant to turn on his light has the opportunity to answer. If he answers correctly, he has the opportunity to answer a "bonus" question which is worth 15 additional points.

This quiz format is very effective for use between teams from different churches or church districts, as well as between teams within a class. Public quizzing competitions motivate students to effective Bible study and learning.

Another idea:

In addition to using Bible quiz questions in this book, a Bible book may be assigned in advance for all contestants to study, and questions

BIBLE BOWL TOURNAMENT

prepared from that book. This procedure encourages youth to read the Bible with a desire to know and understand. The efficiency of their reading will be revealed during the contest. Quiz questions for a particular age group may be compiled over a period of time and used time and again.

6 | Stand By Your Answer

OBJECTIVE: Innovative game tests children's Bible knowledge

Appropriate for ages 6 to 12 • For 4 or more students

Divide the chalkboard into three sections and divide your class into two teams. Prepare a list of Bible quiz questions from your lessons or unit of study, or from those in this book. For each question, you will also need a listing of three answers — preferably one word in length, one of which is the correct answer and the other two false answers.

Before asking the first question, write each answer in one of the sections on the chalkboard. Then ask the first question and have team 1 come to the chalkboard. Each member of the team is to stand in front of the section of the chalkboard they believe has the correct answer. They have five seconds to change their minds as the other team members try to convince them their choice is the correct one.

When the time is up, the teacher says "freeze." Count the number of team members standing in front of the correct answer and give that number of points to that team.

Now write the answers for the next question on the chalkboard sections, read the question, and have team 2's members stand in front of their choices for the answer. Follow the same procedure for determining points earned.

The team ending the game with the most points wins.

Another idea:

If you do not have enough students for teams, let all the children participate in answering each question and award one point to each child who stands in front of the correct answer.

11

7 Balloon Burst

Appropriate for ages 9 to 12 • For 5 or more students

Select enough Bible quiz questions from recent lessons or units of study, or from the questions in this book so there are at least two for each child in the class. Write the questions on small slips of paper. Fold each slip and put it inside a balloon. Blow up the balloons and tie a string to the end of each. Fasten the balloons to a long string stretched across the room. There should be at least two ballons per child.

To play, the children take turns choosing a balloon and breaking it by any means they desire (sitting on it, standing on it, etc.) They must then answer the question hidden inside. If they answer their question correctly they keep the slip of paper. See who ends up with the most slips of paper collected at end of play. The winner(s) could receive a balloon as a prize.

Another idea:
• If you wish, you may provide only one balloon per person. Prepare the question slips by writing a number on each slip of paper. The higher the number the more difficult the question. See who ends up with the highest numbered

question answered correctly. That person is the winner.

The Envelope, Please

OBJECTIVE: Enjoyable quiz format to teach and review any Bible information

Appropriate for ages 6 to 12 • For 4 or more students

Before class, write out Bible quiz questions on one side of index cards and write the answers on the other sides. Each question will be worth 10 points except for one more-difficult question which will have a 25-point value.

Use one envelope for each child in your class. Place one quiz card in each envelope and put all envelopes in a box. Also, make a spinner circle which has the names of all students on it.

(To make a spinner, cut a circle of cardboard and divide into several equal-sized wedges. Write one child's name in each wedge. Attach a large paper clip to the spinner circle as the pointer by running a paper fastener through the clip and into the center of the spinner circle. (See diagram). Tape down the prongs of the paper fastener on the underside of the spinner to prevent scratching.)

To play, the first student may go to the box and pick an envelope. He opens the envelope and reads the question. Then he spins the spinner and calls out the name of the person to which it points. The student whose name was called must answer the question.

If he answers correctly, he earns the designated number of points. He then goes to the box, picks an envelope and follows the above procedure. If he does not answer correctly, the first

player spins again and another name is called. If possible, keep the 25-point question until last. It is exciting to see whose name is called to answer this question and get the high points.

Choose Bible quiz questions from those in this book, or from recent lessons.

9 Bible High Jump

OBJECTIVE: Innovative way to test children's Bible knowledge

Appropriate for ages 9 to 12 • For 4 or more students

To prepare for this quiz, set up a small model of a high jump goal that can be raised to several different lengths. (This could be a 2 by 4 board laid across a stack of books, then across the seats of two chairs and finally across the backs of the chairs.) Prepare a set of Bible questions for each of the different heights. The first set should be easy, and succeeding sets should be progressively more difficult. There should be two questions in each set for each participant. Write out the questions on note paper or index cards and put in separate containers for each of the different difficulty levels.

The first player to "jump" draws a question from the first set. If he answers it he has "cleared the crossbar" placed at its lowest level. (The children may step over the 2 by 4 to show they've moved to the next height.) If he misses he waits until all the other players have tried one question from the first set before he may try a second time. Any participant who fails twice on any set of questions is out.

The remaining participants continue until all the heights are reached or until there is only one participant left. The bar is raised on each new set of questions to show that the difficulty of the questions is greater.

In the event of a tie (two or more remaining players reaching the same height, or the final height being reached by two or more players) additional questions may be asked.

Choose Bible quiz questions from recent lessons or units of study, or from the questions in this book.

10 [Bible Quiz Baseball]

OBJECTIVE: Exciting quiz game motivates Bible learning and review

Appropriate for children ages 9 to 12 • For 4 or more students

Children will eagerly study quiz questions when they know they might hit a home run because they know the correct answers. Choose Bible quiz questions from those in this book or from Bible lessons studied.

Start by choosing one pupil to be the "pitcher." He "pitches" to the pupil at his left (known as the "batter") by asking any Bible quiz question.

The batter must answer the question correctly to make a hit. If he does so within five seconds, and gives the Bible book and chapter where the answer is found, he makes a home run.

If he can answer the question in ten seconds and knows the Bible book, but not the chapter, he makes a three-base hit. If he answers the question in 15 seconds, he makes a two-base hit. If he can tell any correct fact related to the question or answer, even if he cannot give the correct answer, he makes a one-base hit. If he cannot give any correct response to the question, he has made a "strike."

The batter is entitled to try his skill on three "pitches" before he is "out," either by making a run or striking out. He then becomes the next pitcher, and the player on his left becomes the new batter.

A scorekeeper may chalk up the score for each batter — one point for a base-hit, two points for a two-base hit, three points for a three-base hit, and four points for a home run.

If there are enough players, divide into competing teams. Let one team come up to bat and play until three members have struck out. Then let the other team come up to bat. The pitcher should be a member of the other team. Play as many "innings" as time allows. Add up the scores of the players on each team to see which team wins. A pennant or banner with a Bible verse on it would be a nice prize for each player of the winning team (or the player with the most points).

Since this is a very exciting game, and requires knowledge of many Biblical facts, this is a good game to play prior to Sunday school "graduation." Or, hold a "World Series" publicly pitting two classes against each other with each class using a prepared list of quiz questions covering lessons they have learned during the year, or questions from this book.

11 Bible Five Lap

OBJECTIVE: Combines active fun with Bible learning and review

Appropriate for age 9 to teens • For 5 or more students

Arrange the chairs in a circle so the players sit one in front of the other, not side by side. There should be at least twice as many chairs as players. Leave room between the chairs for the players to walk around. Seat the players one behind the other, leaving no empty chairs between the players (approximately half of the circle will be empty).

Make one chair the finish line and the "lap mark." Place a small table or a different type of chair at this point and lay small pieces of note paper on it. As each player passes this table he picks up a piece of paper to show he passed the lap.

To play, players in turn answer Bible quiz questions or name the books of the Bible consecutively. Start with the player at the end of the circle and keep asking the next person in front in line.

If the player answers correctly, he goes to the first empty chair (the empty chair in front of the person at the beginning of the line). If he misses, he stays where he is and the question passes on to the next player.

The players compete to see who can complete five laps first. (It takes approximately two correct answers for a player to complete one lap.)

Choose Bible quiz questions from recent lessons or from those in this book.

12 Musical Chairs Bible Quiz

OBJECTIVE: Inspires Bible learning *and* promptness

Appropriate for ages 6 to 12 • For 5 or more students

Explain to your students one week in advance what is to happen the following week and encourage each class member to pay close attention to the Bible lesson.

Before game time, arrange a line of chairs according to the approximate number of early comers expected. Under several of the chairs tape squares of different colored construction paper.

Five minutes before opening time begin the game; that closes the entries for that week. (The number of on-time or early arrivers will soon increase if you continue to play this game for a short time each week.) Each child should have a chair.

Start playing a record or cassette and have the children march around the chairs. After a few seconds stop the music and have the children sit. Have them check under the chairs for the colored squares. Ask the child with the red square (for instance) a question about last week's Bible lesson, or a Bible quiz question from those in this book. If he cannot answer the question, he must forfeit the square to someone who can.

The second time around, ask for the person having the blue square under his chair to answer a question. If he can, he keeps the square; if not, another child without a square may claim the honor.

Continue until all the squares are claimed. Stop the game for that week.

Label an envelope with each child's name and keep in your classroom. Save the squares from week to week, putting them in the children's

envelopes. At the end of the quarter, or after several weeks, the child with the most collected squares receives a prize or special honor.

As late-comers see the fun of this Bible drill from the sidelines, they will start coming early so they can play too; as non-learners participate they will become intent on listening and learning the Bible lesson each week. The result: all students will learn more Bible facts, and your departmental promptness will improve.

13 Stop & Go Bible Drill

OBJECTIVE: Learn what God says about how we should walk as Christians

Appropriate for ages 10 to 14 • For 4 or more students

Divide the class into two teams, and divide the chalkboard into two sections—one for each team.

One by one, give the references below in Bible drill fashion. The student who finds the Scripture first must stand and read it and then immediately tell if the verse is a "Stop" or a "Go" verse. If he is correct, his team is awarded one point.

You may introduce the drill by saying this: "When we see a red light, we know it means to stop or don't go. When we see a green light, we know we are free to cross the street or to go.

"In the Bible, God has also given us some instructions about stopping and going and about where and when we are to walk. Isaiah said, 'The LORD spoke to me . . . warning me not to follow [walk] the way of this people.' (Isaiah 8:11 NIV) The people in the verse were going when and where God didn't want them to.

"We're going to read some Bible verses about what God wants us to do. If you are the person who finds the verse first, you must tell whether you think the verse is a GO or WALK verse, or if it's a STOP or DO NOT GO verse. If you are correct, your team will get one point."

Stop and Go Scriptures (NIV):

1. 2 John 6 — ". . . Walk in obedience to His commands . . ." GO
2. Proverbs 1:15 — "My son, do not go along with them [sinners] . . ." DO NOT GO or STOP
3. Proverbs 4:14 — "Do not set foot on the path of the wicked or walk in the way of evil men." DO NOT GO or STOP
4. Romans 13:13 — "Behave [walk] decently." GO
5. 1 Thessalonians 2:12 — "Live lives [walk] worthy of God, Who calls you into His kingdom . . ." GO
6. 1 John 1:7 — ". . . Walk in the light, as He is in the light . . ." GO
7. Ephesians 4:17 — ". . . No longer live [walk] as the Gentiles do, in the futility of their thinking." DO NOT GO or STOP
8. Proverbs 22:24 — "Do not make friends with a hot-tempered man, do not associate [go] with one easily angered." DO NOT GO or STOP

9. Luke 21:8 — Jesus said, "Watch out that you are not deceived. For many will come in My name, claiming, 'I am He,' and, 'The time is near.' Do not follow [go after] them." DO NOT GO or STOP
10. Ephesians 5:15 — "Be very careful, then, how you live [walk] — . . . as wise." GO
11. Ephesians 5:8 — "Live [walk] as children of light." GO
12. Ephesians 5:2 — "Live [walk] a life of love, just as Christ loved us . . ." GO
13. Leviticus 20:23 — God said, "You must not live [walk] according to the customs of the nations I am going to drive out before you . . ." DO NOT GO or STOP
14. Leviticus 26:23-24 — God said, "If . . . you do not accept My correction but continue to be [to walk] hostile toward Me . . . I . . . will afflict you for your sins . . ." DO NOT GO or STOP
15. Colossians 2:6 — ". . . As you received Christ Jesus as Lord, continue to live [walk] in Him." GO
16. Proverbs 7:25 — "Do not . . . turn [go] . . . into her [an immoral woman's] paths!" DO NOT GO or STOP

14 | Miracle Rivers Bible Drill

OBJECTIVE: Find several miraculous rivers mentioned in the Bible

Appropriate for ages 9 to 12 • For 4 or more students

Draw a large "M" on the chalkboard as shown in the illustration. Divide each half of the M into 8 spaces. At the point of the M, tape a small envelope in which you have written the Scripture reference "Revelation 22:1" on a sheet of note paper. One side of the M is for recording the rivers found by team 1 and the other side is for recording the rivers found by team 2.

To conduct the drill, divide the class into two teams. One by one, call out the references listed below. The child who finds the verse first reads it aloud and names the river(s). The scorekeeper writes the name of the river in the first square for that team. Continue the drill until one team has all eight squares filled. (A team may move ahead two squares when there are two rivers listed in one verse. Alert the children some rivers are called canals or ravines.)

The child who finds, reads and correctly identifies the eighth river for his team, may open the envelope taped to the board and read the name of the river which is in Heaven. Use this to lead into a discussion of Heaven and what we must do to go to Heaven. Give the plan of salvation and give the opportunity for the children to pray to accept Jesus.

Miracle River Scriptures:
1. Deuteronomy 2:36 (Arnon)
2. Genesis 2:13 (Gihon)
3. Ezekiel 1:1 (Chebar)
4. Judges 4:7 (Kishon)
5. Genesis 2:14 (Hiddekel and Euphrates)
6. Mark 1:5 (Jordan)
7. 2 Kings 5:12 (Abana and Pharpar)
8. Ezra 8:31 (Ahava)
9. Jeremiah 2:18 (Sihor)
10. 2 Kings 17:6 (Habor)
11. Psalm 65:9 (River of God)
12. 2 Kings 5:14 (Jordan)

15 Tic-Tac-Toe Bible Quiz

OBJECTIVE: A new way to play an old game and review Bible facts

Appropriate for ages 9 to 12 • For 6 or more students

Divide the class into two teams. One will be the "X" team and the other will be the "O" team. Draw the familiar tic-tac-toe framework on the chalkboard. As members of the teams correctly answer Bible quiz questions, as asked by the teacher, an "X" or "O" can be marked on the board until one team gets three marks in a row.

Variety can be introduced into the quiz by using masking tape to mark the tic-tac-toe grid on the floor. (Make each square about 2 feet across.) As a team player responds with the correct answer, he can stand in one of the marked squares. When a team has three players standing in a row, they win the game.

Choose Bible quiz questions from recent lessons or from the questions in this book.

---

16 Grow A Flower Bible Drill

OBJECTIVE: Exciting drill inspires team cooperation in Scripture search

Appropriate for ages 9 to 12 • For 4 or more students

These Bible verses make an exciting Bible drill. The team which finds the verse first is awarded the stem of a flower which is drawn on the chalkboard. (All players on one team must find the Scripture before the players on the other team.) Read the verses aloud.

As each team continues to score points, draw a leaf, another leaf, the flower center and then the petals. The first team to "grow a flower," wins!

Suggested Bible Verses:

2 Peter 3:18	Psalm 119:11
Philippians 1:6	Colossians 3:16
Hebrews 5:12	Hebrews 4:12
1 Peter 2:2	James 1:22
John 15:5	2 Timothy 4:2
1 Timothy 4:12	1 Peter 2:2
2 Timothy 2:15	Psalm 119:1-5

17 Open The Book

Appropriate for ages 9 to 12 • For 8 or more students

Divide the class into two teams by having the pupils count off 1, 2, 1, 2, etc. Have all the 1s form a team and the 2s form another team. Ask them to stand in two lines facing each other.

The teacher hands the first player in each line a Bible and says, "When the whistle blows you are to open the Bible, find this verse of Scripture (give the same verse to both players), read it aloud, close the Bible, hand it to the next player in line and ask him to find and read a verse of Scripture. Continue until the person at the end of the line has read his Scripture, whereupon he must close the Bible and pass it back through the line to the first player."

The teacher (and a helper for the second team) should see that each player actually finds and completely reads his verse. The first team who gets the Bible back to the first player wins the contest.

Choose Scripture verses from recent lessons or from those in this book.

Another idea:

Rather than have each player choose the Scripture verse which the next player finds and reads, the teacher could prepare the Bibles in advance by putting small Post-it notes on the Bible page, listing the next verse to be read.

For example, if the first player reads John 3:16, on that page of the Bible, the teacher would place a note saying the second player is to read

John 1:12. After the first player has completed reading John 3:16, he closes the Bible, hands it to the second player and tells him to find and read John 1:12.

By preparing the Bibles for both teams in advance in this manner, each team finds and reads the same verses and has equal chances of winning.

18 Find The Point Bible Drill

OBJECTIVE: Develops Bible reading comprehension skills

Appropriate for ages 10 to 14 • For 8 or more students

This Bible drill will challenge the students to quickly find, read, comprehend and then answer questions about a passage of Scripture.

Divide the class into teams. Give the first Bible passage reference. The first student who finds it may stand and read it, then close his Bible and sit down with the rest of the students. (Award one point to the reader's team.)

Then one by one, ask the questions listed for each passage and award one point for each correct answer given. If no one can answer a question, you could give the reference again and give one point for the student who can find the correct answer first.

After all the questions about a particular passage have been answered, discuss the significance of the Bible lesson and what we can learn from it.

Find The Point Scriptures:

1. Read Daniel 1:1-15
    a. What were some of the "good points" King Nebuchadnezzar was looking for in the young men chosen to be taught the Babylonian language? (They should be strong and healthy, intelligent, have knowledge in many fields, alert and sensible, able to serve or teach.) (Award one point for each answer, up to 4 points.)
    b. What did the king order the young men to be fed? (They were to be given the king's food and wine.)
    c. What was Daniel's reaction to the order? (Daniel refused to eat the king's food.)
    d. Did Daniel prove his point by not eating the king's food? (Yes)
    e. How did Daniel and his friends look in comparison with those who did eat what the king ordered? (They were fatter and healthier)
    f. What "good point" did Daniel display in this story? (Self-control)
    g. What quality do we need for self-control? Daniel had it too. (Determination)

2. Read Genesis 13:1-11
    a. What was Abram rich in? (Livestock, silver and gold) (Award one point for each answer; possible 3 points.)
    b. Why was it necessary for Abram and Lot to split up and go separate ways? (They had so much the land couldn't hold it all; there was fighting among the herdsmen.) (2 points)
    c. Why was Abram's suggestion to separate a good one? (It would stop the fighting and cause better feelings.)
    d. What choice did Abram give Lot? (If Lot went left, Abram would go right; if Lot went right, Abram would go left.)
    e. What did Lot do before choosing? (Lot looked over the country in order to choose the best.)
    f. What "good point" did Abram display in this story? (Unselfishness)
    g. What can we learn not to do from Lot? (Always pick the best for ourselves.)

3. Read 1 Samuel 19:1-7
    a. What one word describes Jonathan and David? (Friends)
    b. What did Jonathan do to prove he was David's friend? (Jonathan told David to hide from his father until morning.)
    c. How did Jonathan stick up for David in talking to his father? (Jonathan told his father how good David had been to him.)

d. What event in David's past did Jonathan remind his father of? (Jonathan reminded his father of the time David killed the giant and saved all of Israel.)
e. Did Saul listen to Jonathan's talk about David? (Yes)
f. What was Saul's decision about David? (He shouldn't be killed.)
g. What did Jonathan do in order to let David know?(Jonathan called David and told him what his father had decided; he brought David to Saul.) (2 points)
h. What two points about Jonathan were brought out in this story? (Jonathan was a good friend and was willing to prove it.) (2 points)

19 Who And How?

OBJECTIVE: A creative quiz for students on Bible events and why they happened

Appropriate for age 9 to teens • For 4 or more students

Divide the class into two or three teams. Starting with the first person on the first team, ask the following "Who and How" questions. (You may also use other quiz questions in this book, or prepare your own questions from recent lessons or units of study.)

Award each team five points if the player answers the "who" part of the question correctly, and give ten points if the team answers the "how" or "why" part of the question. Give one point if either question can be answered only after looking up the Scripture reference listed.

If a team cannot answer the question, the other team has an opportunity to do so. The second question is then asked to the first person on the second team. The team with the most points at the end of the quiz is the winner.

Who and How Quiz Questions:
(These questions may also be used with other Bible quiz formats in this book.)

1. Who helped cause the walls of Jericho to fall? How? (Joshua; the sound of the trumpets — Joshua 6:20)
2. What group of people did God feed in the wilderness? How? (Israelites; manna from Heaven — Exodus 16:15)
3. What rich publican devised a unique way to get to see Jesus in the crowd? Where did he go? (Zacchaeus; climbed a sycomore tree — Luke 19:1-4)
4. Who escaped an angry mob by going over a wall? How? (Paul; basket lowered by friends — Acts 9:22-25)
5. Who tried to run away from God and was thrown overboard during a storm? How did he get back to shore? (Jonah; in the belly of a great fish — Jonah 1 and 2)
6. Who did Elisha say would be healed of leprosy if he followed directions? What were the instructions? (Naaman; dip seven times in Jordan River — 2 Kings 5:9-10)
7. Who was punished for praying to his God? How? (Daniel; thrown into the lions' den — Daniel 6)
8. What strong man killed a thousand Philistines? How? (Samson; with the jawbone of a donkey — Judges 15:16)
9. Who descended upon the disciples on the Day of Pentecost? How was this evidenced? (Holy Spirit; tongues of fire — Acts 2:1-4)
10. Who was the prophet that had an unusual "ride" to Heaven? How? (Elijah; chariot of fire — 2 Kings 2:11)
11. Who traveled with a floating zoo? How? (Noah; built the ark — Genesis 7)
12. Who did Jesus comfort while in a boat on rough waters? How? (disciples; stilled a storm — Luke 8:22-25)

20 Bible Library

OBJECTIVE: Challenging questions from every book of the Bible

Appropriate for age 10 to teens • For 4 or more students

Prepare a set of 66 miniature books according to the pattern below. (Another easier way to make the miniature books is to use 66 standard 4 by 6 inch index cards, folding them according to the pattern below. You do not need to cut the index cards down in size.)

Print the name of one book of the Bible on the "back" or spine of each miniature book so all the Bible books are represented.

On the inside of each of the books, print the question from the list on pages 26 and 27 concerning something from the particular Bible book. Also print the chapter which gives the answer. (Answers follow each question and can be used as the answer key, or you may wish to prepare a separate answer key for a quick reference to the correct answers.) Other questions from each book may be substituted for the questions listed below.

To play, stand up the miniature books on a table and divide the class into two teams. Each team takes turns having a member choose a Bible book and answer the question therein. If the answer given is correct, the team gets to keep that book. If the answer given is incorrect, the other team is given an opportunity to answer the question. If they answer correctly, they get to keep the book. If neither team answers correctly, that book goes back on the table. At the end of the quiz, the team with the most books collected wins.

Other ideas:
• This quiz could be organized so a team can

keep on choosing books and answering questions as long as they make no mistakes. When they do make a mistake, the other team gets a chance to answer that question and then may choose books and answer the questions until they make a mistake.
• Point values could be assigned to each Bible book so that teams which correctly answer questions about less familiar books are awarded more points than for questions about familiar books and subjects.

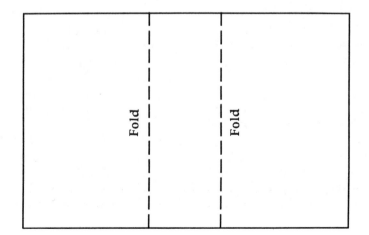

Continued on next page . . .

Continued . . .

Books of the Bible Quiz Questions:

(These questions may also be used with other Bible quiz formats in this book.)

Genesis — What man did God say would be the "father of many nations"? Genesis 12 (Abram).

Exodus — Who led his people into idolatry by making the golden calf? Exodus 32 (Aaron).

Leviticus — Who were the two men that were slain because they offered strange fire before the Lord? Leviticus 10 (Nadab and Abihu).

Numbers — What were the names of the two spies who gave a good report of the land of Canaan? Numbers 14:6-7 (Joshua and Caleb).

Deuteronomy — What great man died and was buried by the Lord in a valley in the land of Moab? Deuteronomy 34 (Moses).

Joshua — What was the name of the woman who protected the spies Joshua sent and who was rescued when her city was captured? Joshua 2 (Rahab).

Judges — What judge over Israel determined the will of God by putting out the fleece of wool on the floor? Judges 6 (Gideon).

Ruth — What was the name of the man of great wealth who took Ruth to be his wife? Ruth 4 (Boaz).

1 Samuel — Who was the young prince of Israel that gave up his right to the throne because of his great love for God's anointed choice? 1 Samuel 18 (Jonathan).

2 Samuel — What was the name of David's handsome son who rebelled against his father and sought the throne of Israel? 2 Samuel 15 (Absalom).

1 Kings — What king was known as the wisest man in all the world? 1 Kings 3 (Solomon).

2 Kings — Who was the prophet of the Lord that caused the iron axe head to swim? 2 Kings 6 (Elisha).

1 Chronicles — Who was the king of Israel that fell upon his sword and was killed? 1 Chronicles 10 (Saul).

2 Chronicles — What king of Judah offered incense upon the altar in the sanctuary and was stricken with leprosy? 2 Chronicles 26:19 (Uzziah).

Ezra — Who was the king of Persia that made the proclamation for the Israelites to return to Jerusalem? Ezra 1 (Cyrus).

Nehemiah — What was the name of the priest who read the book of the law before the people in the city of Jerusalem? Nehemiah 8 (Ezra).

Esther — Who was the man who prepared the gallows for Mordecai and was hanged upon it himself? Esther 7 (Haman).

Job — Who was Job's accuser before the Lord, and tempted Job to forsake God? Job 1 (Satan).

Psalms — Who was known as the "sweet psalmist of Israel" and wrote most of the psalms in this book? Psalm 3 (David).

Proverbs — What great king of Israel wrote the Book of Proverbs? Proverbs 1 (Solomon).

Ecclesiastes — What is the name of the king of Israel who wrote this book? Ecclesiastes 1 (Solomon).

Song of Solomon — Who does the Rose of Sharon symbolize as written about by Solomon in this song? Song of Solomon 2 (Christ, the Messiah).

Isaiah — Who was the king whom Isaiah told he was going to die? After Isaiah prayed God added fifteen years to the king's life? Isaiah 38 (Hezekiah).

Jeremiah — Who was the mighty king of Babylon Jeremiah prophesied would take Israel captive? Jeremiah 25 (Nebuchadrezzar).

Lamentations — Who was the "weeping prophet" who lamented the sins of Israel? Lamentations 1 (Jeremiah).

Ezekiel — Who was the prophet of God who walked through the valley of dry bones? Ezekiel 37 (Ezekiel).

Daniel — What were the names of the three children of Israel cast into the fiery furnace? Daniel 3 (Shadrach, Meshach, and Abednego).

Hosea — What was the name of Hosea's wife, whom he brought back from slavery? Hosea 1 (Gomer).

Joel — The prophet Joel was the son of whom? Joel 1 (Pethuel).

Amos — Who was the high priest that complained against Amos to the king? Amos 7 (Amaziah).

Obadiah — Who was the brother of Jacob, against whose descendants Obadiah prophesied? Obadiah 6 (Esau).

Jonah — From Whom did the prophet Jonah flee in a ship bound for the city of Tarshish? Jonah 1 (The Lord).

Micah — Who was it that Micah foretold would be born in the city of Bethlehem? Micah 5 (Christ the Messiah).

Nahum — Who was the prophet who preached in Nineveh, the ruins of which Nahum tells about? Nahum 3 (Jonah).

Habakkuk — To Whom did Habakkuk cry out against the iniquity of the people? Habakkuk 1 (The Lord).

Zephaniah — Zephaniah prophesied during the reign of what man, who became king at eight years of age? Zephaniah 1 (Josiah).

Malachi — What prophet did Malachi say God would send before the coming of the "great day of the Lord"? Malachi 4 (Elijah)

Matthew — What wicked king plotted to kill the baby Jesus? Matthew 2 (Herod).

Mark — Who were the two men that appeared with Christ in His transfiguration? Mark 9 (Moses and Elias).

Luke — What was the name of the criminal who was released instead of Christ? Luke 23 (Barabbas).

John — Lazarus, whom Jesus raised from the dead, was the brother of what two women? John 11 (Mary and Martha).

Acts — What disciple of the Lord baptized the Ethiopian eunuch? Acts 8 (Philip).

Romans — Through whom did the apostle Paul say sin entered the world? Romans 5 (Adam).

1 Corinthians — Who was the brilliant preacher who helped Paul preach the Gospel and "water" the spiritual seeds sown? 1 Corinthians 3:16 (Apollos).

2 Corinthians — Who was the man whom the apostle Paul sent to the church at Corinth to straighten out matters? 2 Corinthians 8 (Titus).

Galatians — Who was the apostle with whom Paul dwelt fifteen days in Jerusalem after his conversion? Galatians 1 (Peter).

Ephesians — With what beloved brother and faithful minister did Paul send this letter to the church at Ephesus? Ephesians 6 (Tychicus).

Philippians — Paul said there were saints in the household of this man who lived in the city of Rome. Who was he? Philippians 4 (Caesar).

Colossians — Who was the beloved physician, whose greetings Paul sent to the church at Colosse? Colossians 4 (Luke).

1 Thessalonians — About Whose coming again did Paul write to the saints at Thessalonica? 1 Thessalonians 4 (Christ's).

2 Thessalonians — Whose salutation is given as the token in the letter to the Thessalonians? 2 Thessalonians 3 (Paul's).

1 Timothy — Who was "Paul's own son in the faith" and pastor of the church at Ephesus? 1 Timothy 1 (Timothy).

2 Timothy — Who was it that forsook Paul, "having loved this present world"? 2 Timothy 4 (Demas).

Titus — Who was the lawyer whom Paul asked Titus to bring with him? Titus 3 (Zenas).

Philemon — Who was the unprofitable servant whom Paul asked Philemon to take back? Philemon (Onesimus).

Hebrews — Who was the priest of the most high God to whom Abraham paid tithes? Hebrews 7 (Melchisedec).

James — James, the writer of this epistle, says if anyone lacks wisdom, he should ask Whom? James 1 (God).

1 Peter — Peter speaks of Abraham's wife as an example of obedience. Who was she? 1 Peter 3 (Sarah).

2 Peter — Who does Peter call a "preacher of righteousness"? 2 Peter 2 (Noah).

1 John – Who killed his brother for jealousy? 1 John 3 (Cain).

2 John — To whom was this second letter from the apostle John written? 2 John 1 (The elect lady).

3 John — The third epistle of John is addressed to three persons, Gaius, Diotrephes, and whom? 3 John 12 (Demetrius).

Jude — Who was the archangel that contended with the devil over the body of Moses? Jude 9 (Michael).

Revelation — Who do we read in Revelation is to be bound a thousand years in the bottomless pit? Revelation 20 (Satan).

21 Bible Scavenger Hunt

OBJECTIVE: Creative activity teaches Bible research skills

Appropriate for age 9 to teens • For 4 or more students

No doubt your students have participated in a scavenger hunt where everyone goes seeking all sorts of odd things. This Bible drill lets them try their skill at locating peculiar objects found in the Bible.

In the drill, the objects to be found will suggest various Bible stories to the students. The Bible stories in turn will bring to mind the book of the Bible where the story is found, and so on, until the students locate where the object is mentioned in the Bible.

A Bible concordance can be used along with the Bible to give the students practice in using it to help locate Scriptures.

For this activity, duplicate the activity sheet from page 29 for each student. Allow the students to work individually (if you have a concordance for each student) or in small groups. As the students find the place where the object is mentioned in the Bible, they are to write the reference on the line. They are to also list the person associated with the object. When all have finished or a predetermined time has elapsed, let the students give the reference they found for each object. A small prize, perhaps "scavenged" from a thrift shop, could be given to the winner(s).

Another idea:

Conduct this drill by reading aloud to the students the object to be found. The students then begin locating the object in the Bible. The first person who finds the chapter and the verse in which the object is found stands or raises his hand and gives the reference and person associated with the object. Points can be given as the verses are found, and the winner may be awarded a prize.

Answers to Bible Scavenger Hunt:
1. Judges 6:37 — Gideon
2. John 2:6 — Jesus
3. Genesis 44:2 — Benjamin
4. 1 Samuel 17:40 — David
5. Matthew 3:4, or Mark 1:6 — John the Baptist
6. John 20:7 — Jesus
7. John 6:9 — Little boy
8. Exodus 3:2 — Moses
9. Matthew 2:11 — Wise Men
10. Matthew 3:4 or Mark 1:6 — John the Baptist
11. Genesis 19:26 — Lot's wife
12. Matthew 13:31 — Jesus
13. Genesis 37:3 — Joseph
14. Ephesians 6:17 — Me

BIBLE SCAVENGER HUNT

Can you find these things in the Bible? If you can, write on the lines the book, chapter and verse where you found the object in the Bible. Also write the name of the person associated with the object.

1. A fleece of wool _____

_____

2. Six waterpots of stone _____

_____

3. Silver cup in a sack of grain _____

_____

4. Five smooth stones _____

_____

5. Raiment of camel's hair _____

_____

6. A wrapped napkin _____

_____

7. Five barley loaves and two small fishes _____

_____

8. A burning bush _____

_____

9. Gold, frankincense, and myrrh _____

_____

10. Locusts and wild honey _____

_____

11. A pillar of salt _____

_____

12. A grain of mustard seed _____

_____

13. A coat of many colors _____

_____

14. The helmet of salvation _____

_____

22 **The Game Of Kings**

OBJECTIVE: Innovative way to learn the kings of Israel and Judah

Appropriate for ages 9 to 12 • For 2 or 4 players

The names and order of the kings of Israel and Judah are very confusing to learn. Very few Bible teachers are able to tell which kings were of Israel or Judah without a long, tedious search through Kings and Chronicles. This game will help to familiarize your students (and you) with these kings. It should be played often enough to fix the names of the kings in memory.

Make four copies of page 31 containing 10 king cards. Glue two sheets to one color of poster board (these will be the kings of Judah) and glue the other two sheets to poster board of a different color (these will be the kings of Israel). Label each king with his name, number and nation from the list below. (See sample card below.) Cut out each card.

To play, one player takes all the kings of Israel, and the other player takes all the kings of Judah, mixes them up, and lays them face down on the table. The first player takes the top card and displays it. The second player does likewise. The player whose card has the highest number takes both cards. Play continues in this manner until all kings have been played. Count the cards, and award the players one point for each card won.

If four people want to play, divide the cards evenly, and give half of the set to the partner. If two cards of the same number should be played at the same time, they will go to the one who first presented the card.

13.	Joash (Jehoash)	17.	Menahem
14.	Jeroboam 2	18.	Pekahiah
15.	Zechariah	19.	Pekah
16.	Shallum	20.	Hoshea

Kings of Judah

1.	Rehoboam	11.	Jotham
2.	Abijah	12.	Ahaz
3.	Asa	13.	Hezekiah
4.	Jehoshaphat	14.	Manasseh
5.	Jehoram (Joram)	15.	Amon
6.	Ahaziah (Azariah)	16.	Josiah
7.	Athaliah	17.	Jehoahaz (Shallum)
8.	Joash (Jehoash)	18.	Jehoiakim
9.	Amaziah	19.	Jehoiachin
10.	Azariah (Uzziah)	20.	Zedekiah

Kings of Israel

1.	Jeroboam 1	7.	Omri
2.	Nadab	8.	Ahab
3.	Basasha	9.	Ahaziah
4.	Elah	10.	Joram
5.	Zimri	11.	Jehu
6.	Tibni	12.	Jehoahaz

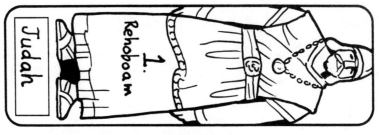

Sample card
(DO NOT USE)

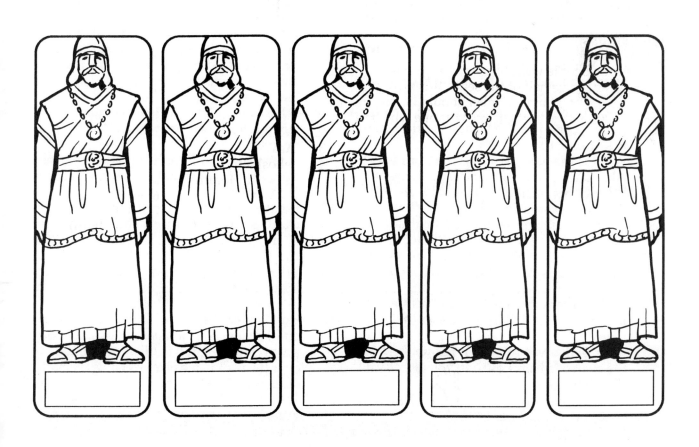

23 Bible Geography Quiz

OBJECTIVE: Reviews places and events of the Bible

Appropriate for age 9 to teens • For 4 or more students

This Bible quiz is an appropriate conclusion to a Bible geography project or unit of study. It is also excellent to challenge your student's knowledge of Bible places and events anytime.

Enlarge the map on page 33 by using an enlarging copy machine, an overhead projector or redraw the map outline and location dots onto a large sheet of paper.

Point to the correct location on the map and ask the corresponding quiz question below. (If the quiz is being used at the conclusion of a Bible geography study, you may add more locations to the map on page 33 and prepare more quiz questions.)

Give one point for each correct answer given. The team or child with the most points wins.

Bible Geography Quiz Questions:

(You may also use these questions with other Bible quiz formats in this book.)

1. Can you give the name of this body of water west of Palestine? (Mediterranean Sea)
2. What is the name of this city from which Paul and Barnabas set forth on their missionary journey? (Antioch)
3. What is this famed river called, flowing into the Dead Sea? (Jordan)
4. From what sea does the Jordan River flow? (Sea of Galilee)
5. What is the name of this city just over the Jordan, conquered by Joshua and the Israelites? (Jericho)
6. What is the name of this place from which Abraham set out? (Ur of the Chaldees)
7. What is this great river in the land where the Israelites were held in bondage? (Nile)
8. What is the name of this mountain of importance in Jewish history? (Mount Sinai)
9. What was the name of the city in Assyria where Jonah was sent to preach repentance? (Nineveh)
10. What is the name of this village near Jerusalem, the home of Mary and Martha? (Bethany)
11. Near Bethany is this town known best for the birth of a baby boy. Can you identify it? (Bethlehem)
12. Can you identify this city where Solomon built the temple? (Jerusalem)
13. What name was given to this place where Jacob slept and dreamed of the ladder to heaven? (Bethel)
14. What is the name of this city where Jesus preached in the Synagogue and healed a man possessed by the devil? This was also the hometown of Peter, Andrew, James and John. (Capernaum)
15. What is the name of this mountain where Elijah defeated the prophets of Baal? (Mount Carmel)
16. After Mary and Joseph and Jesus returned from Egypt, they went to live in this town. (Nazareth)
17. What were the names of these two cities God destroyed because of their wickedness after rescuing Lot and his family? (Sodom and Gomorrah)
18. What was the name of this town where Jesus performed His first miracle by turning water into wine? (Cana)
19. Saul was converted to Christianity and his name changed to Paul here. He also avoided people who wanted to kill him by escaping over the wall in a basket. What is the name of this city? (Damascus)
20. The Jordan River flows into this body of water which is known for its high content of salt and minerals. (Dead Sea)

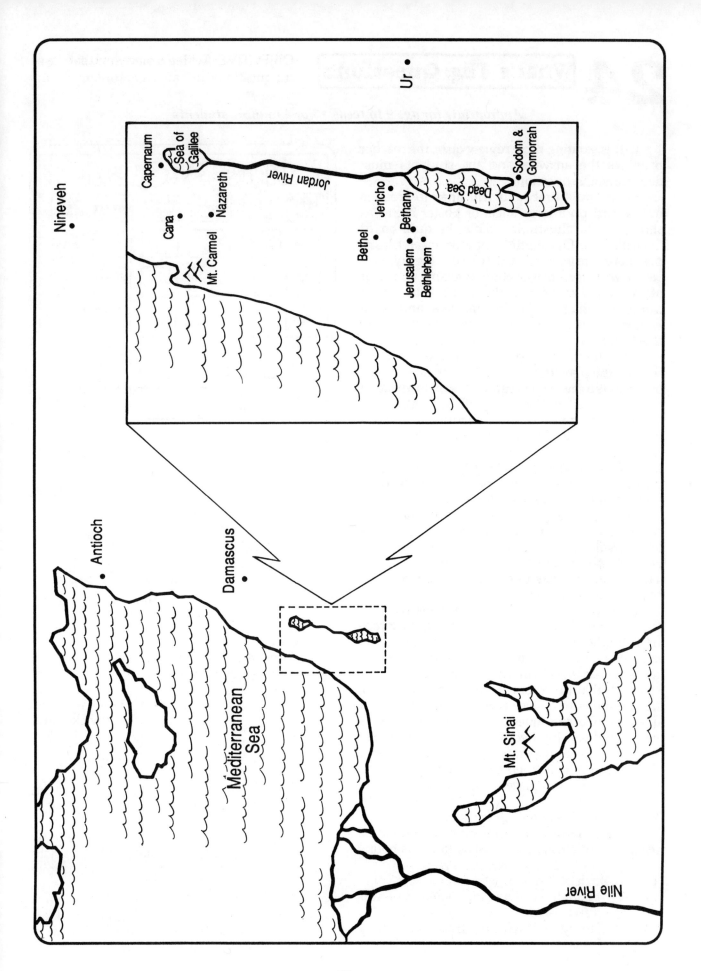

24 What's The Question?

OBJECTIVE: A Bible review quiz that mixes up questions and answers for lots of fun

Appropriate for age 9 to teens • For 3 or more students

In this exciting Bible review quiz, the teacher provides the answers and the students must determine the questions.

Before quiz time, you will need to create a quiz board on a large sheet of poster board as shown in the illustration. Title the quiz board "What's The Question?" Tape 36 clear plastic pockets to the poster board. (Use double layers of Saran wrap or clear acetate available at art or office supply stores to make the pockets.) Insert cards, on which the topics, answers, and point values are printed, into the pockets, as shown in illustration.

Place the topic cards face out so they can be seen by the players, but the answer cards should be turned so the players cannot see them ahead of time. (The back of the cards will be blank.)

Use the questions and categories which follow, or use other questions in this book. You can also create your own questions and categories from recent lessons or units of study. The higher the number of points, the more difficult the question should be under each topic.

To begin the quiz, the first player chooses a category and point value. The teacher (or quiz leader) will remove the answer card of that category and point value and read the question aloud. The player then has 10 seconds to respond with the correct "question."

If he gives the correct question, he receives the number of points for the card and may continue by choosing another card. When a question is given incorrectly, anyone else in the class can raise his hand and attempt to "question the answer." If that person gives the correct question, he continues to choose cards until he misses a question. (Correct "questions" follow the answers below and can be used as the key, or you may wish to prepare a separate key for quick reference during the quiz.) When the correct response is given, the card is replaced in the pocket face out.

What's The Question? Quiz Questions:

(These answers and questions may also be used with other Bible quiz formats in this book.)

TOPIC: Birth of Jesus
10 pts.   Bethlehem — In what small city was Jesus born?
20 pts.   Herod — What king tried to kill baby Jesus?

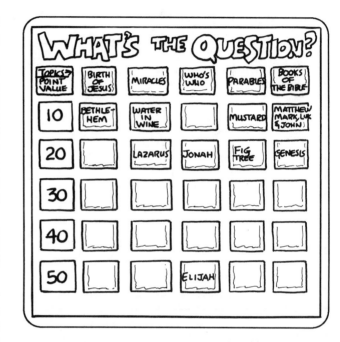

30 pts.   Savior — What is meant by the name Jesus?
40 pts.   The song of a multitude of the heavenly host — What song did the shepherds hear?
50 pts.   Mary kept all these things, and pondered them in her heart — What did Mary do about all the things the shepherds told?

TOPIC: Miracles
10 pts.   Water into wine — What was Jesus' first miracle performed at a wedding in Cana?
20 pts.   Lazarus — Who was the brother of Mary and Martha that Jesus raised from the dead?
30 pts.   "Thy sins be forgiven thee" — What did Jesus say to the paralytic man brought to be healed.
40 pts.   "O thou of little faith, wherefore didst thou doubt?" — What did Jesus say to Peter when he began to sink while walking on the water?
50 pts.   "How much then is a man better than a sheep?" — What did Jesus ask the Pharisees when they tried to accuse Him of unlawfully healing on the sabbath?

TOPIC: Who's Who

10 pts. Daniel — Which prophet was a close friend of three young men who were thrown into the fire?

20 pts. Jonah — Who had a frightening experience with a great fish while on the way to Nineveh?

30 pts. Noah — Who found grace in the eyes of the Lord?

40 pts. Barabbas — What criminal was released instead of Jesus?

50 pts. Elijah — Who was the prophet known as the Tishbite?

TOPIC: Parables

10 pts. Mustard — Jesus taught that we should have faith like what kind of seed?

20 pts. Fig tree — What kind of tree did Jesus use as an example of bearing fruit?

30 pts. The vine — Jesus said we are the branches and He is the ?

40 pts. The tares — What did Jesus say is burned in the fire and "so shall it be in the end of this world"?

50 pts. Laborers in the vineyard — What parable did Jesus tell to teach that the last shall be first, and the first last?

TOPIC: Books of the Bible

10 pts. Matthew, Mark, Luke and John — What books are called "The Gospels"?

20 pts. Genesis — What is the first book of the Bible?

30 pts. Acts — Which book tells about the rapid spread of Christianity following Jesus' death and resurrection?

40 pts. Revelation — Which book tells about the Second Coming of Christ?

50 pts. Hebrew and Greek — What was the original language of the Old Testament; what was the original language of the New Testament?

Appropriate for age 9 to teens

Use these intriguing questions with the Bible quiz formats in this book, or organize your quiz as follows:

Divide the class into teams. Beginning with the letter A, read the clue to the first player on the first team who must give the correct answer. The first player on the second team must give the answer to the clue for B.

If a player cannot give the correct answer, he must forfeit his turn on the next round. The team who successfully gives the most correct answers is the winner.

Other ideas:
- Write the alphabet on the chalkboard or on a worksheet and have the students fill in the correct names as you give the clues.
- Give 5 points if the question can be answered without the use of the Bible. If a student cannot answer the question, he may ask the teacher to give him the Scripture reference where the answer is found. If he can find the answer in the Bible within 30 seconds, he gets 1 point, rather than forfeiting his turn.

ABC Bible Quiz Questions:

A   The father of the Hebrew nation. (Abram — Genesis 12:1, 2)

B   A blind man whom Jesus healed. (Bartimaeus — Mark 10:46)

C   One of the two faithful spies that spied out Canaan. (Caleb — Numbers 14:6)

D   A king who was a man after God's own heart. (David — Acts 13:22)

E   A priest who trained little Samuel. (Eli — 1 Samuel 2:11)

F   A governor who called Paul mad. (Festus — Acts 26:24)

G   A giant who was killed by a stone. (Goliath — 1 Samuel 17:49, 21:9)

H   One of Noah's sons. (Ham — Genesis 9:18)

I   The name God gave Jacob. (Israel — Genesis 32:28)

J   The forerunner of Jesus. (John the Baptist — Matthew 3:1-3)

K   The name of King Saul's father. (Kish — 1 Samuel 9:3)

L   The beloved physician who traveled with

Paul. (Luke — Colossians 4:14)

M   Born a slave, but became a prince. (Moses — Exodus 2:5, 6, 10)

N   A Syrian general who was a leper. (Naaman — 2 Kings 5:1)

O   A prophet who wrote one short message. (Obadiah)

P   The disciple who betrayed Jesus but later repented. (Peter — Luke 22:54-62)

Q   What Esther became. (Queen — Esther 2:17)

R   David's great grandmother. (Ruth — Ruth 4:17)

S   Abraham's wife. (Sarah — Genesis 17:15)

T   A young preacher to whom Paul addressed two of his letters. (Timothy)

U   He died for touching the ark of the covenant. (Uzzah — 2 Samuel 6:6, 7)

V   The one who was queen before Esther. (Vashti — Esther 2:17)

W   What Jesus is sometimes called. (The Way — John 14:6)

X   What Jesus set; and we are to follow. (Example — 1 Peter 2:21 or John 13:15)

Y   What we are to take upon us when we learn of Christ. (His yoke — Matthew 11:29)

Z   The father of John the Baptist. (Zacharias — Luke 1:13)

26 Bible Land Train

OBJECTIVE: Reviews Bible places and events

Appropriate for ages 9 to 12 • For 4 or more students

Your students are sure to enjoy this imaginary train trip through Bible lands.

Draw a map outline of Israel on the chalkboard. The first player goes to the board and says the name of a city or destination and places it correctly on the map. (Locations such as mountains, rivers, lakes and such may be used as well as cities.) The second player goes to the board, names another location, places it on the map and then draws a line to that location from the first location.

For more fun and challenge, have each child tell about the location he puts on the map, or about an event that happened there or a person who lived there.

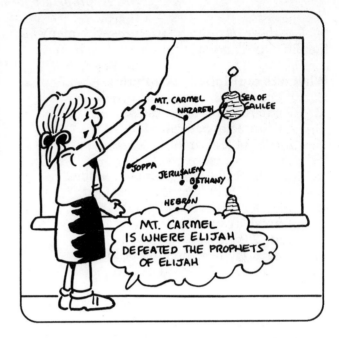

27 A Visit To The Old Testament

OBJECTIVE: This active quiz reviews stories of Old Testament Bible characters

Appropriate for ages 8 to 11 • For 4 or more students

Before quiz time, write each of the names below on a sheet of note paper. As the children come to class, safety pin one of the note paper sheets to each child's back without him seeing the name.

Each child must go to another child and ask no more than two yes-or-no questions to try to figure out who he is. He may then ask another child two more questions and so on until he identifies himself.

Abraham	Ruth
Moses	Esther
Joshua	Samuel
Jacob	David
Isaac	Goliath
Samson	Noah
Gideon	Daniel
Sarah	Elijah

28 Bible Multiplication Drill

OBJECTIVE: Learn about spiritual multiplication in the Bible

Appropriate for age 10 to teens

Use these intriguing Scriptures with many of the Bible drill and quiz formats in this book.

What was multiplied? Scriptures:
1. Genesis 47:27 (people of Israel)
2. Deuteronomy 11:21 (days)
3. 1 Chronicles 5:9 (cattle)
4. Job 27:14 (children)
5. Psalm 16:4 (sorrows)
6. Isaiah 59:12 (transgressions, or sins)
7. Ezekiel 35:13 (words against God)
8. Hosea 2:8 (silver and gold)
9. Daniel 4:1 (peace)
10. Jude 2 (peace and love)
11. Acts 6:1, 7 (the disciples or followers)
12. Acts 12:24 (the Word of God)

29 Bible Arithmetic

OBJECTIVE: Brain teasers that help reinforce important Bible numbers

Appropriate for age 9 to teens • For 1 or more students

Duplicate the activity sheet on page 39 for each student. Have the pupils try to solve the problems without the use of their Bibles and give each student with the correct answer 10 points. Then let the students use their Bibles and award five points for every correct answer. Give a small prize to the person(s) with the highest points.

Answers:

Problem 1:
$30 + 40 + 30 \div 10 - 2 = 8$

Problem 2:
$40 \div 10 + 2 = 6$

Problem 3:
$12 + 7 + 6 - 5 = 20$

BIBLE ARITHMETIC

Try solving these problems without using your Bible. Then use your Bible to check your answers or look up the numbers you don't know.

Problem 1

The number of silver pieces for which Jesus was betrayed
(Matthew 26:15) _____

Add the sum of days Jesus was seen after His Resurrection
(Acts 1:3) + _____

Add the age of Jesus when He was baptized
(Luke 3:21-23) + _____

Divide this by the number of silver pieces a woman had
(Luke 15:8) ÷ _____

Subtract from this the number of commandments on which hang all the law and the prophets
(Matthew 22:36-40) − _____

Total. You will have the number of the Victory Chapter of Romans. What chapter is it? = _____

Problem 2

The number of years that the Israelites tempted God
(Hebrews 3:9) _____

Divide this by the number of lepers Jesus cleansed at one time
(Luke 17:17) ÷ _____

Add to this the number of angels that were seen at the tomb of Jesus
(Luke 24:4) + _____

Total. You will have the number of the chapter in Matthew where the Lord's Prayer is located. What chapter is it? = _____

Problem 3

The number of legions of angels Jesus could have called to his aid
(Matthew 26:53) _____

Add the number of churches in John's day
(Revelation 1:4) + _____

Add the number of brethren who accompanied Peter after his vision
(Acts 11:12) + _____

Subtract from this the number of coverings over the tabernacle
(Exodus 35:6) − _____

Total. You will have the number of the chapter in Exodus where the Ten Commandments are found. What chapter is it? = _____

30 Bible Sheep Search

OBJECTIVE: Learn what God says about His followers

Appropriate for age 9 to teens

When studying about the Good Shepherd, the following questions and references make an excellent Bible quiz which shows what God says to us about His sheep.

Use these questions and Scripture references with the Bible quiz formats in this book or invent your own way of quizzing.

Sheep in the Bible Quiz Questions:

1. What should the sheep of God's pasture give to Him forever? Thanks — Psalm 79:13
2. What did Jesus say a man would do if he had 100 sheep and one went astray? Leave the 99 and go looking for the lost sheep — Matthew 18:12
3. Who was it that led Joseph like a shepherd would lead a flock of sheep? Shepherd of Israel — Psalm 80:1
4. What does a shepherd do when he finds his lost sheep? Rejoices — Luke 15:5
5. Who are the sheep of God's pasture? We are — Psalm 100:3
6. How are we like sheep? We have gone astray — Isaiah 53:6
7. Why do sheep follow their shepherd and not someone else? Because they know their shepherd's voice — John 10:4-5
8. When Jesus talked about the sheepfold, what did He say He was? The door — John 10:9
9. What does the shepherd carry that is a comfort to the sheep? Rod and staff — Psalm 23:4
10. What does the Good Shepherd give for His sheep? His life — John 10:11
11. Like whom did Isaiah prophesy that Jesus would feed His flock? Like a shepherd — Isaiah 40:11
12. When Jesus saw the multitudes, He was moved with compassion because they were scattered abroad like _____? Sheep —

Matthew 9:36

13. Who came to the shepherds who were abiding in the fields by night? The angel of the Lord — Luke 2:9
14. Jesus told His disciples that He sent them forth like sheep in the midst of _____? Wolves — Matthew 10:16
15. What does a hired shepherd do when he sees a wolf coming? He leaves the sheep and flees — John 10:12
16. What did the shepherds say to each other in Luke 2:15? "Let us now go even unto Bethlehem, and see this thing which is come to pass, which the Lord hath made known unto us."
17. What did Jesus say He had to bring in John 10:16? Other sheep which are not of this fold.
18. What did Jesus say He gives to His sheep? Eternal life — John 10:28

31 Animals and Birds Quiz

OBJECTIVE: Learn about interesting animals and birds in the Bible

Appropriate for age 9 to teens

Following are several facts and references about animals and birds in the Bible. Use these facts and references with the Bible quiz formats in this book, or invent your own way of quizzing.

Bible Animals Quiz Questions:
1. They were smaller than wolves and noted for their craftiness. Boys chased them out of the vineyards: Foxes (Song of Solomon 2:15)
2. They are sometimes called rock rabbits and live in the hills among the rocks: Conies (Proverbs 30:26)
3. Another name for the animal chased by hunters in our forests: Hart (Psalm 42:1)
4. Travelers ride these animals across the desert: Camel (Genesis 24:63-64)
5. David used a club to fight these two animals that attacked his father's sheep: Lion and bear (1 Samuel 17:34-35)
6. This animal is a ferocious, spotted cat: Leopard (Isaiah 11:6)
7. Pharoah had a dream about seven fat ones and seven thin ones: Cows (Genesis 41:1-4)
8. In Bible times, this animal was a symbol of military power: Horses (Isaiah 31:1)
9. John the Baptist called Jesus, "The _____ of God." Lamb (John 1:29)
10. The Prodigal Son left his father's home and fed these animals: Swine (Luke 15:15)

Bible Birds Quiz Questions:
1. A large web-footed bird with a long beak: Pelican (Psalm 102:6a)
2. A bird of prey often seen soaring in the sky: Hawk (Job 39:26)
3. A bird with beautiful plumage: Ostrich (Job 39:13-16)
4. The coming of these birds was considered a sign of spring: Turtle dove (Song of Solomon 2:12)
5. Two of these birds were sold for a farthing: Sparrow (Matthew 10:29)
6. A bird resembling the quail: Partridge (Jeremiah 17:11)
7. God's people ate manna and this bird when they wandered in the wilderness: Quail (Exodus 16:12-13)
8. King Solomon kept these beautiful birds in his palace: Peacocks (2 Chronicles 9:20-21)
9. These birds brought Elijah food to eat: Ravens (1 Kings 17:6)
10. Immediately after Jesus was baptized, the Spirit of God came down from heaven in the form of this bird: Dove (Matthew 3:16)

32 Did You Know That?

OBJECTIVE: Bible quiz questions about interesting Bible facts

Appropriate for age 9 to teens

Following is a list of 60 questions about some very interesting facts in the Bible. They are phrased and planned to create interest in Bible study.

These questions may be used with the Bible quizzes in this book, or divide them up so just a few questions are used each week. You can also "challenge" your students to look up the answers to one or two questions at home during the week.

Did You Know That? Quiz Questions:
1. Who was swallowed up in the earth? Why?(Korah, Datham, and Abiram, they rebelled against Moses; Numbers 16:1-32)
2. In what place did hailstones help to win a battle? (Bethhoron; Joshua 10:11)
3. What army lost a victory because of a thunder storm? (The Philistines; 1 Samuel 7:10)
4. Who made iron to swim? (Elisha; 2 Kings 6:1, 5-7)
5. What bitter waters were made sweet? (The waters of Marah; Exodus 15:23-25)
6. What wicked grandmother gained the throne by having all her relatives she could find killed? (Athaliah; 2 Chronicles 22:10-12)
7. What young man went to sleep in a meeting and fell out of the window and died, but was resurrected? (Eutychus; Acts 20:9)
8. What country would the Lord wipe as a man wipes dishes? (Jerusalem; 2 Kings 21:13)
9. What woman was in government service and had her office under a palm tree? (Deborah; Judges 4:4, 5)
10. What man had a bed 13 1/2 feet long and 6 feet wide? (Og, king of Bashan; Deuteronomy 3:11)
11. Who was it that had twenty-four fingers and toes? (A giant from Gath; 2 Samuel 21:20)
12. What chapter has four verses just alike? Quote the verse. (Psalm 107; Oh that men would praise the LORD for His goodness, and for His wonderful works to the children of men!)
13. What is the shortest chapter in the Bible? (Psalm 117)
14. What verse in the Bible has all the letters of the alphabet except "J" and "Q"? (Esther 2:14)
15. How many of the disciples did Paul see? Which ones? (Two, Peter and James; Gala-

tians 1:18, 19)
16. Where did Abraham plant a grove? (Beersheba; Genesis 21:33)
17. Who had a sickness that was healed by a fig cake? (Hezekiah; 2 Kings 20:1-7)
18. A man put two sticks on a fire and a snake jumped out and fastened itself on his hand. Who was the man? What happened? (Paul; he shook the snake off into the fire. Acts 28:3-5)
19. Where was the first temple built in Israel? (Jerusalem; 1 Kings 12:25-33)
20. What ornament did Solomon say should grace the neck of a child? (Instruction of the father and law of the mother; Proverbs 1:8, 9)
21. Where in the Bible does it tell about spotted horses? (Zechariah 1:8)
22. Who wrote a book for the second time? (Jeremiah; Jeremiah 36:28)
23. Who was the man no one would believe? (Jeremiah; Jeremiah 18:18)
24. Who found a strange book? (Hilkiah; 2 Kings 22:8-10)
25. Who were put in stocks? (Jeremiah, Paul, and Silas; Jeremiah 20:2; Acts 16:19-24)
26. Who built a gallows for another man and was hanged upon it himself? Why? (Haman, to pacify the king; Esther 7:10)
27. Who gave a poor beggar something better

than money? What? (Peter, made a lame man whole; Acts 3:6)

28. Who was put into a deep well for punishment? What had he done wrong? (Jeremiah, the princes did not like his prophecy; Jeremiah 38:1-6)

29. Who was the man who kept an enraged mob from killing some of the apostles? He was a Pharisee. (Gamaliel; Acts 5:34, 35)

30. Who was the man that boasted himself to be somebody and had a following of four hundred men? He was slain. Who told this story in the Bible? (Theudas, Gamaliel; Acts 5:36)

31. This woman had two names. She did social work. Who was she? What did she do? (Tabitha or Dorcas, she did good works; Acts 9:36-41)

32. This man was a false prophet—a sorcerer. He tried to turn a leader away from following the true way. Who was he? Who prevented him from turning the leader away? (Elymas, Saul [Paul]; Acts 13:6-9)

33. What was another name for Gideon? (Jerubbaal; Judges 7:1)

34. Two detectives heard a dream explained which gave them courage. Who were the two men? What did they do? (Gideon and Phurah, worshipped God and defeated the Midianites; Judges 7:10-23)

35. When was honey sent as a present? To whom? (When there was a famine, Joseph; Genesis 43:1, 11, 15)

36. Where in the Bible is it said horses are swifter than eagles? (Jeremiah 4:13)

37. Who was a commissioner to the Israelites east of the Jordan? (Phinehas; Joshua 22:13-32)

38. Where in the Bible is it told that women painted their faces? (2 Kings 9:30, Jeremiah 4:30)

39. Who were the doorkeepers of the ark? (Obed-edom and Jehiah; 1 Chronicles 15:18, 24)

40. Who concealed 100 prophets in a cave? Why? (Obadiah, because Jezebel wanted to kill them; 1 Kings 18:3, 4)

41. Who was chief of the temple musicians? (Asaph; 1 Chronicles 25:1-2)

42. Who used a nail as a weapon to kill a man? (Jael; Judges 4:21)

43. Who was an overseer of David's storehouse? (Jehonathan; 1 Chronicles 27:25)

44. What priest married an idolatrous wife? (Ezra; Ezra 10:16-18)

45. Who were called to imitate making the rod into a serpent? (wise men, sorcerers, magicians; Exodus 7:11)

46. Who had a house made of ivory? (Ahab; 1 Kings 22:39)

47. Who was entrusted with the priesthood starting in the tabernacle? (Aaron and his sons; Exodus 40:12-15)

48. Who was forbidden to grieve over the death of their two brothers? (Eleazar and Ithamar; Leviticus 10:1-7)

49. What father was about to kill his son until God stopped him? (Abraham; Genesis 22:1-14)

50. Where did Aaron die? (Mount Hor; Numbers 20:22-29)

51. Where in the Bible is the practice of gossip forbidden? (Leviticus 19:16, Psalm 50:20, Proverbs 11:13, Proverbs 20:19, Ezekiel 22:9)

52. Name some games found in the Bible. Do you think you would have fun playing them? (Racing – 1 Corinthians 9:24; Running – Galatians 2:2; Running or boxing – 1 Corinthians 9:26; Fighting – 2 Timothy 4:7)

53. What false prophet was punished with blindness? (Elymas; Acts 13:8, 10, 11)

54. Who was the Queen of Ethiopia? (Candace; Acts 8:27)

55. Was Rachel's grave marked? Where was it located? (Yes, with a pillar, in Bethlehem; Genesis 35:19-20)

56. When was blindness inflicted upon the Sodomites? Why? (Because they were trying to attack the two angels in Lot's house; Genesis 19:1-11)

57. A father commanded his son to draw a sword but the son feared to obey. Who were the father and son? (Gideon and Jether; Judges 8:13, 20)

58. What were the names of the two leaders who lived in Samaria whose names differed by one letter? (Elijah and Elisha; 1 Kings 19:19)

59. What lad was crowned king at the age of eight years? (Josiah; 2 Kings 22:1)

60. Where was the first miracle in the New Testament performed? (Cana; John 2:1-11)

33 | Going Fishing Bible Drill

OBJECTIVE: Learn what you need to go fishing

Appropriate for ages 9 to 12

Each of the Scriptures below tell about fishing in the Bible. The student who first finds the verse should read it aloud and tell what was used to catch the fish.

Going Fishing Scriptures:
1. Isaiah 19:8 (angling nets)
2. Habakkuk 1:15 (angling nets)
3. Amos 4:2 (fishhooks)
4. Job 41:7 (spears)
5. Ezekiel 26:5, 14 (nets)
6. Matthew 4:18 (nets)
7. Luke 5:4 (nets)
8. John 21:6 (nets)

---

34 | Where Did It Happen?

OBJECTIVE: Rhyming clues reveal the places important Bible stories happened

Appropriate for ages 8 to 12

Duplicate the Where Did It Happen? activity sheet on page 45 for each child.

The children are to unscramble the letters in each rhyming clue to find out where the Bible event happened. Then they are to print the name of the city next to the corresponding number on the map.

Answers:
1. Damascus; 2. Capernaum; 3. Cana; 4. Nazareth; 5. Jericho; 6. Jerusalem; 7. Bethany; 8. Bethlehem.

Where Did It Happen?

Unscramble the mixed-up word in each rhyming clue to find out where the Bible story happened. Then write the name of the place next to the corresponding number on the map. See how many you can get without using your Bible. Then look up the Bible verses to check you work.

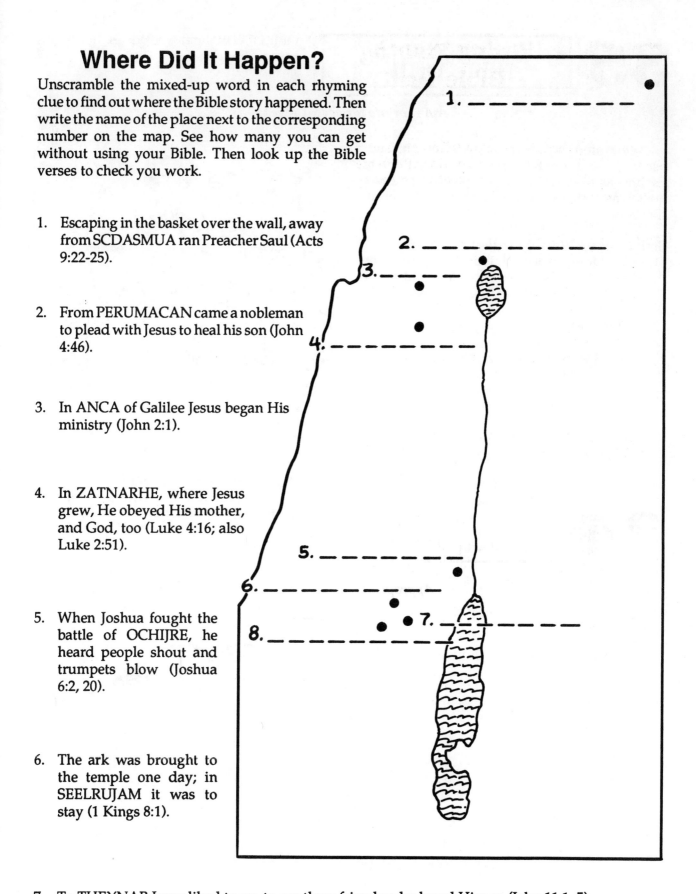

1. Escaping in the basket over the wall, away from SCDASMUA ran Preacher Saul (Acts 9:22-25).

2. From PERUMACAN came a nobleman to plead with Jesus to heal his son (John 4:46).

3. In ANCA of Galilee Jesus began His ministry (John 2:1).

4. In ZATNARHE, where Jesus grew, He obeyed His mother, and God, too (Luke 4:16; also Luke 2:51).

5. When Joshua fought the battle of OCHIJRE, he heard people shout and trumpets blow (Joshua 6:2, 20).

6. The ark was brought to the temple one day; in SEELRUJAM it was to stay (1 Kings 8:1).

7. To THEYNAB Jesus liked to go, to see three friends who loved Him so (John 11:1, 5).

8. The Saviour of the world was born in THEMELHEB, on Christmas morn (Luke 2:4-6).

45

35 | Psalm Search Bible Drill

OBJECTIVE: Find Scriptures in Psalms concerning worship

Appropriate for age 9 to teens

When studying about ways to worship God, use these Scripture references, all in the Book of Psalms, as the basis for a Bible drill. Use these questions with the different Bible drill formats in this book, or invent your own drill.

Scriptures on Worship in Psalms:

1. In what two places should people praise the Lord? In His sanctuary (church) and in the firmament (anywhere in God's universe) — Psalm 150:1
2. Where was the Psalmist glad to go? Into the house of the Lord — Psalm 122:1
3. How should we come before the presence of the Lord? With singing — Psalm 100:2
4. What kind of song were the people to sing in the congregation of the saints (in church)? A new song — Psalm 149:1
5. What special way were the people to worship the Lord? With a joyful noise — Psalm 100:1
6. Name two instruments that could be used to make a joyful noise: Trumpets and cornet — Psalm 98:6
7. Not only does God want us to praise Him with joyful noise, but when we worship, God said for us to do what also? Be still, and know that I am God. — Psalm 46:10
8. The Psalmist said, "Let us worship and ____" Bow down (kneel before the Lord) — Psalm 95:6

9. What were the people told to bring when they came into the Lord's courts of worship? An offering — Psalm 96:8
10. What did the Psalmist tell God he would not forget? Thy Word — Psalm 119:16
11. What did the Psalmist say he would rather be than to live in wickedness? A doorkeeper in the house of my God — Psalm 84:10
12. How are we to worship the Lord? In the beauty of holiness — Psalm 96:9

46

36 Give Unto The Lord Drill

OBJECTIVE: Scriptures teach tithing and stewardship

Appropriate for age 9 to teens

The Scriptures below are excellent to assist you in teaching about the subject of stewardship or tithing. For a Bible drill, give the references and see which student can find the Scripture first. Then have all the students read the verse together for further emphasis.

These verses may also be used with other Bible drills in this book, or invent your own contest.

Scriptures on Giving and Tithing:
1. What did Jesus say about giving in Acts 20:35? — It is more blessed to give than to receive.
2. What kind of giver does God love? A cheerful giver. — 2 Corinthians 9:7.
3. In Matthew 10:8, Jesus said because we have received _____ , we should give _____ . — Freely.
4. How much should we give? Every man shall give as he is able, according to the blessing of the LORD thy God which He hath given thee. — Deuteronomy 16:17
5. What is the least we should give? One tenth of our income. — Genesis 28:22
6. How are our gifts accepted? "According to that a man hath, and not according to that he hath not" — 2 Corinthians 8:12
7. What does the Bible say about being boastful in our giving? Do not your alms before men, to be seen of them. — Matthew 6:1
8. What is a good rule for giving? Do it with

simplicity. — Romans 12:8
9. How often should we give? Each week, on the first day of the week (Sunday). — 1 Corinthians 16:2
10. Where should we bring our tithes? The storehouse (the house of God). — Malachi 3:10
11. What is promised to liberal givers? Give, and it shall be given unto you . . . with the same measure that ye mete withal it shall be measured to you again. — Luke 6:38

37 — Search For Peace

OBJECTIVE: Learn what God's Word says about peace

Appropriate for age 9 to teens

The following questions review many different Scriptures regarding peace. Use these questions with the Bible quiz formats in this book, or invent your own way of quizzing.

Search For Peace Quiz Questions:

1. With what will the Lord bless His people? Peace — Psalm 29:11
2. Through whom do we have peace with God? Our Lord Jesus Christ — Romans 5:1
3. Who did Jesus say shall be called the children of God? Peacemakers — Matthew 5:9
4. In what state will God keep the person whose mind is stayed on God? Perfect peace — Isaiah 26:3
5. In this verse, when does the Lord promise to give peace: "Now the Lord of peace Himself give you peace"? Always — 2 Thessalonians 3:16
6. The peace of God passes _____? All understanding — Philippians 4:7
7. Paul tells the Romans to follow after the things that make for _____? Peace — Romans 14:19
8. With whom are we to follow peace? All men — Hebrews 12:14
9. Whose peace should we let rule in our hearts? The peace of God — Colossians 3:15
10. With whom did Paul tell the Thessalonians to be at peace? Yourselves — 1 Thessalonians 5:13
11. Jesus told His followers about the things to come, so "that in Him" they might have _____? Peace — John 16:33
12. What did Paul want "the very God of peace" to do for the people to whom he was writing? Sanctify you wholly — 1 Thessalonians 5:23

38 Who Said it? Quiz

Appropriate for age 9 to teens

Read the following Scriptures dealing with holiness. If a student can give the name of the person who said or wrote the words, he will receive five points. An additional five points will be given if he can give the chapter and verse where the quote is found. A Scripture verse plaque would be a nice prize for each of the winners.

Who Said It? Quiz Questions:
1. "For this is the will of God, even your sanctification." Paul — 1 Thessalonians 4:3.
2. "Be ye therefore perfect, even as your Father which is in heaven is perfect." Jesus — Matthew 5:48.
3. "Follow peace with all men, and holiness, without which no man shall see the Lord." Writer to the Hebrews, probably Paul — Hebrews 12:14.
4. "Sanctify them through thy truth; thy word is truth." Jesus — John 17:17.
5. "Purge me with hyssop, and I shall be clean; wash me, and I shall be whiter than snow." David — Psalm 51:7.
6. "But as He which hath called you is holy, so be ye holy in all manner of conversation." Peter — 1 Peter 1:15.
7. "Draw nigh to God, and He will draw nigh to you. Cleanse your hands, ye sinners; and purify your hearts, ye double-minded." James — James 4:8.
8. "Wherefore, beloved, seeing that ye look for such things, be diligent that ye may be found of Him in peace, without spot, and blameless." Peter — 2 Peter 3:14.
9. "And every man that hath this hope in Him purifieth himself, even as He is pure." John — 1 John 3:3.
10. "By the which will we are sanctified through the offering of the body of Jesus Christ once for all." Writer to the Hebrews — Hebrews 10:10.

39 Mother's Day Quiz

OBJECTIVE: Learn about some of the women in the Bible

Appropriate for age 9 to teens

These intriguing questions about women in the Bible are ideal for an exciting quiz on Mother's Day, or any other day.

Some basic questions to discuss with your students in relation to these women, or any other study of Biblical characters, are:

• Why do you think this person's story is in the Bible?

• What purpose or lesson did the Holy Spirit mean for us to learn by this person's story?

• What can I learn from her experience or story?

Use these intriguing questions with the Bible quiz formats in this book, or invent your own way of playing.

Women of the Bible Quiz Questions:

1. I prayed for a son and when God answered my prayer, I gave my son to the Lord. Who am I? (Hannah — 1 Samuel 1, 2.)
2. I overheard a conversation between my husband and an angel which made me laugh. Who am I? (Sarah or Sarai — Genesis 18:9-15.)
3. A great king arranged to have my husband killed in battle so that he could marry me. Who am I? (Bathsheba — 2 Samuel 11.)
4. I robbed a man of his strength by giving him a haircut. Who am I? (Delilah — Judges 16:4-22.)
5. I was greatly loved by my daughter-in-law. Who am I? (Naomi — Ruth 1:7-18.)
6. An angel said to me, "Fear not . . . thou hast found favour with God." Luke 1:30 Who am I? (Mary — Mother of Jesus)
7. I saved my people from destruction by finding favor with my husband, the king. Who am I? (Esther — Esther 4:11-5:2)
8. As a young widow, I attracted the attention of my future husband while gleaning in his fields. Who am I? (Ruth — Ruth 2:1-13)
9. I listened to a serpent in a garden. Who am I? (Eve — Genesis 3:1-7)
10. My husband was unable to speak throughout my pregnancy. Who am I? (Elizabeth — Luke 1:18-22, 55-66)
11. I was distressed because my sister did not help with the work when Jesus was a guest in our home. Who am I? (Martha — Luke

10:38-42)

12. I conspired with one of my twin sons to deceive his father. Who am I? (Rebekah — Genesis 27:1-17.)
13. My occupation caused me to be known as a "seller of purple." Who am I? (Lydia — Acts 16:14, 15.)
14. I anointed the feet of Jesus with ointment and dried them with my hair. Who am I? (Mary, sister of Martha — John 12:1-8.)
15. I mistakenly thought my risen Lord was the gardener as I looked at Him through tears. Who am I? (Mary Magdalene — John 20:11-18.)
16. I was a prophetess and a judge of the children of Israel before they were ruled by kings. Who am I? (Deborah — Judges 4:4)
17. To earn the right to marry me, my husband worked for seven years; because my father deceived him and gave him my sister instead, he worked an additional seven years. Who am I? (Rachel — Genesis 29:16-30)
18. Because my mistress was angry at me and my son, we were sent out into the wilderness. An angel rescued us and promised God would make my son a great nation. Who am I? (Hagar — Genesis 21:9-20.)

OBJECTIVE: Interesting facts to learn about fathers in the Bible

Appropriate for age 9 to teens

How about a special quiz to learn about many of the fathers in the Bible? Use these intriguing questions with the Bible drills and quizzes in this book, or invent your own way of playing.

Fathers of the Bible Quiz Questions:
1. What father built the great Temple in Jerusalem? Solomon — 1 Kings 8:22
2. What father had two fishermen sons who became Jesus' followers? Zebedee — Matthew 4:21
3. What man was called the father of his people? Abraham — Genesis 18:18
4. What father came to Jesus to ask Him to heal his sick daughter? Jairus — Luke 8:41
5. What father was the first man? Adam — Genesis 2:20
6. What father was the first king of Israel? Saul — 1 Samuel 19:1
7. What father had twin sons and was deceived by one of them? Isaac — Genesis 27:22
8. What father went from sling to throne? David — 2 Samuel 5:25
9. What father was sold as a slave boy but became a great statesman? Joseph — Genesis 37:28
10. What father became speechless until his son was born? Zacharias — Luke 1:13
11. What father heard God speak through a burning bush? Moses — Exodus 3:3
12. What father was the first sailor? Noah — Genesis 6:9

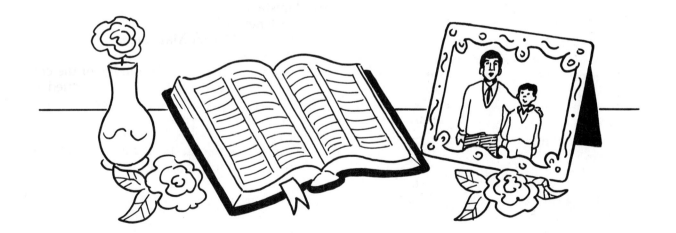

41 Joseph Quiz

OBJECTIVE: Interesting facts about one of God's heroes

Appropriate for age 9 to teens

These intriguing questions about Joseph will get your students hunting the Scriptures. All the answers can be found in Genesis chapters 37-50. Ask your students the questions, and allow them to search in these chapters for the answers.

These questions can also be used with the many Bible drills and quizzes in this book.

Joseph Quiz Questions:

1. Who was Jacob's favorite son? Joseph.
2. Why was he the favorite of Jacob? He was the son of Jacob's old age.
3. Who was Joseph's grandfather? Isaac. Who was his great-grandfather? Abraham.
4. How many brothers did Joseph have? How many sisters? 11 brothers and one sister.
5. Why were his brothers jealous of Joseph? They disliked the favor their father paid him.
6. What was the main idea of Joseph's dream? That someday Joseph's brothers would bow down to him.
7. What did the brothers plan to do with Joseph when he came to visit them in the fields? At first they planned to kill him, but Reuben protested; so they put him in a pit. Then they decided to sell him.
8. What did the boys tell their father? They dipped Joseph's coat in a kid's blood, showed it to Jacob, and asked him to identify it. Jacob thought a wild animal had killed Joseph.
9. Where was Joseph taken? Egypt.
10. Who purchased him? Potiphar, an officer of the Pharaoh.
11. Did Potiphar trust Joseph? Yes.
12. Why was Joseph cast into prison? Potiphar's wife said false things about him and convinced her husband they were true.
13. Two men had dreams that Joseph interpeted. Who were they? Butler and baker.
14. How long did Joseph remain in prison? Two years.
15. The Pharaoh had dreams which Joseph inter-preted. What did they mean? They meant that there would be seven fat years and seven lean years.
16. What did Joseph tell Pharaoh he must do after Joseph interpreted the dreams? He must store up food for seven years until the years of famine. If he did this there would be enough food.
17. Who did Pharaoh set up as the leader in collecting the grain? Joseph.
18. Who came to buy food in Egypt? Joseph's brothers.
19. What did Joseph do when he recognized them, but they did not recognize him? At first he treated them harshly, and at last he told them who he was.
20. What did Joseph insist his brothers do? Bring Benjamin to Egypt.
21. Did Joseph ever see his father again? Yes, he was finally reunited with him and Isaac lived to see Joseph's sons.

42 — Names For Jesus

OBJECTIVE: Learn names the Bible uses to describe Jesus, our Savior

Appropriate for age 9 to teens

Each of these 20 Scriptures contains a word or words which are names of Jesus. You should find 22 different names.

These Scriptures may be used with other Bible drills and quizzes in this book also.

Names for Jesus Scriptures:
1. 1 John 4:14 — Son; Saviour of the world.
2. Zechariah 9:9 — King
3. John 1:29 — Lamb of God
4. John 14:6 — The Way
5. Isaiah 9:6 — Wonderful
6. John 10:11— The Good Shepherd
7. Isaiah 7:14 — Immanuel
8. Isaiah 9:6 — Counsellor
9. John 1:1 — The Word
10. John 14:6 — The Truth
11. Luke 7:34 — Son of Man
12. 1 Timothy 1:12 — Lord
13. Isaiah 9:6 — The Mighty God
14. Isaiah 59:20 — Redeemer
15. Daniel 9:25 — Messiah the Prince
16. John 14:6 — The Life
17. Isaiah 9:6 — The Everlasting Father
18. John 1:9 — The True Light
19. Romans 11:26 — The Deliverer
20. Isaiah 9:6 — Prince of Peace
21. Matthew 1:23 — Emmanuel

43 Where Were They Born? What Did They Do?

OBJECTIVE: Questions about the birth and careers of important Bible people

Appropriate for age 9 to teens

Answer the following questions about the Bible people listed below:
- Where were they born?
- What were their professions?
- What can we learn from their lives and stories?
- Why do you think their story is in the Bible?

One by one give the name of each Bible person below to your students. Award five points for each question above which they answer without the use of a Bible, and give one point if a Bible is needed. A small prize can be given to the winner, if desired.

These Scripture references and questions can be used with other Bible drill and quiz formats in this book also.

Where were they born? What did they do? Quiz Questions:
1. Moses: Birthplace: Egypt — Exodus 1:1, 2:1, 2; Profession: Shepherd — Exodus 3:1.
2. Abraham: Birthplace: Ur of the Chaldees — Genesis 11:27-28; Profession: Rich in cattle, silver and gold — Genesis 13:2.
3. Ruth: Birthplace: Moab — Ruth 1:4; Profession: Gleaner — Ruth 2:17.
4. Samuel: Birthplace: Ramathaimzophim — 1 Samuel 1:1, 2, 20; Profession: Prophet of the Lord — 1 Samuel 3:20.
5. Paul: Birthplace: Tarsus — Acts 22:3; Profession: Tentmaker — Acts 18:3.

44 Who Cheated?

OBJECTIVE: Learn about tricky deceivers in the Bible and the results of their actions

Appropriate for age 9 to adults

According to the dictionary definition, "cheating" means "to get something from another by dishonesty or trickery."

The Bible tells about many people who tried some of these tricks, and cheated others. Read these questions to your students and see if they can answer them without using their Bibles. Then see if they can find the Bible book, chapter and verse where the answer is.

Other questions for the students to answer are: What was the result of this person's cheating? Did he or she repent of their sin? If so, what happened? Points may be given for each answer.

These questions about Bible cheaters can also be used with the other Bible drills and quizzes in this book.

Who Cheated? Quiz Questions:

1. What respected Bible character cheated his brother out of his birthright and had to run for his life because of it? Jacob — Genesis 27:18-46

2. What New Testament believer had been a cheat while in government employment, but promised to repay what he had stolen after he met Jesus? Zacchaeus — Luke 19:1-8

3. Which of Jesus' companions pretended to be concerned about the poor, but really was cheating His master out of money? Judas — John 12:4-6

4. What king of Israel demanded high taxes from his people in order to provide himself and his pals with plenty of spending money? Rehoboam — 1 Kings 12:1-14

5. What handsome young man tried to steal the kingdomship from his own father, even though it would have meant death for the popular king? Abaslom — 2 Samuel 15:2-14

6. What man cheated in taking forbidden things into his tent, and caused the defeat of Israel? Achan — Joshua 7:11-22

45 | What's My Name?

OBJECTIVE: Exciting clues reveal important Bible characters

Appropriate for age 9 to teens

Your students are sure to enjoy the challenge of identifying these Bible characters. Read the clues to the class, pausing slightly between each so the students may guess the person.

The clues are designed to be more difficult at the beginning, with each successive clue becoming easier. If a student can correctly identify the Bible person on the first clue given, the student earns six points. If guessed on the second clue, he earns five points, and so on.

These quizzes may be used one per week or use all the Bible people in one longer quiz. Keep a running score of the points earned for each individual Bible person to determine the winner when all the individual quizzes have been completed. There are both long quizzes and short quizzes included, with Scripture references.

What's My Name? Quiz Questions:

1. I was one of the early Christian disciples and my name significantly means "crown." (Acts 6:1-5)
    By the power of the Holy Spirit I was enabled to do great wonders and miracles among the people. (Acts 6:8)
    I am spoken of in the Scriptures as a man "full of faith and of the Holy Ghost." (Acts 6:5)
    I was chosen as one of seven to serve tables in the daily ministration. (Acts 6:2-5)
    I was accused by false witnesses of blaspheming both God and Moses. (Acts 6:11)
    I was cast out of the city and stoned to death by my accusers. (Acts 7:58) Who am I?
    Stephen

2. My mother was a Jewess but my father was a Greek. (Acts 16:1)
    I was a disciple from the city of Lystra in Asia Minor. (Acts 16:1)
    I accompanied the apostle Paul on his second missionary journey. (Acts 16:3)
    Paul, imprisoned in Rome, asked me to bring him his cloak and the books, but especially the parchments. (2 Timothy 4:13)
    Paul called me his "own son in the faith." (1 Timothy 1:2)
    Paul spoke of my unfeigned faith, which dwelt first in my grandmother Lois and in my mother Eunice. (2 Timothy 1:5) Who am I?
    Timothy

3. At my birth my mother said, "I have gotten a man from the Lord." (Genesis 4:1)
    When I grew up I became a farmer, a tiller of the ground. (Genesis 4:2)
    I built a city and named it after my first son. (Genesis 4:17)
    I dwelt in the land of Nod, a fugitive and a vagabond upon the earth. (Genesis 4:12, 16)
    After committing a terrible sin, I said unto the Lord, "My punishment is more than I can bear." (Genesis 4:13)
    I killed my own brother, and became the first murderer. (Genesis 4:8)
    Who am I?
    Cain

4. I was a fisherman, of the city of Bethsaida, a disciple of Jesus. (Matthew 4:18)
    John the Baptist first introduced me to Jesus. (John 1:40)
    I went and found my brother and brought him to Jesus. (John 1:41-42)
    My brother and I forsook our nets and followed Him. (Mark 1:18)
    Jesus said to me and my brother, "Follow Me, and I will make you fishers of men." (Matthew 4:19)
    My brother was Simon Peter. (Matthew 4:18)
    Who am I?
    Andrew

5. I was a woman of Galilee, and a follower of Jesus. (Matthew 27:55)
    Joanna and Susanna, and I ministered unto Christ of our substance. (Luke 8:2, 3)
    The Lord had delivered me from seven evil spirits. (Luke 8:2)
    I was with other women at the cross who had followed Jesus from Galilee. (Matthew 27:55, 56)
    I came with Mary and Salome, on the first day of the week, with spices to anoint His body. (Mark 16:1)
    The Lord appeared first to me after His resurrection, and called me by name. (Mark 16:9)
    Who am I?
    Mary Magdalene

Shorter questions:

6. I am a young man who traveled with Paul. I grew tired of the sacrifices we had to make. I loved the world more than the work we were doing. I left Paul and the others and went to Thessalonica. Who am I?
    Demas — 2 Timothy 4:10.

7. I am also a young man who traveled with Paul. I, too, left the work and went home to Jerusalem. When I wanted to go with Paul on his next trip, he didn't want me to go. Who am I?
    John Mark — Acts 15:37-39.

8. I am a man who came to Jerusalem from a far country. While I was returning home, I was reading a scroll of the book of Isaiah. A man named Philip explained the meaning of what I had read about the Messiah. He baptized me, and I went on my way rejoicing. Who am I?
    The Ethiopian eunuch — Acts 8:34-39.

9. I pursued Christians from city to city, and brought them as prisoners back to Jerusalem. One day, on the road to Damascus, the Lord appeared to me. I began to understand that I had been doing wrong in persecuting the Christians. I was baptized, and began preaching Christ Jesus as Lord. I preached on Mars Hill in Athens. Who am I?
    Saul/Paul — Acts 9:1-18.

10. We are a husband and wife who helped Paul establish churches in several places. We also helped a preacher named Apollos to understand the way of the Lord in a better way. Paul lived and worked with us because we shared the same profession of tentmakers. Who are we?
    Aquila and Priscilla — Acts 18:26.

11. I was Paul's right-hand man on his second missionary journey. Once in a dark prison cell, while we sang songs, God sent an earthquake. We saved the jailer from taking his own life, and we preached Christ to him. Who am I?
    Silas — Acts 16:25-34.

12. I am a business woman of the town of Philippi. While I was in a prayer meeting along a riverside, Paul turned my heart to faith in Jesus as the Son of God. I was Paul's first convert to Jesus Christ in Europe. Who am I?
    Lydia — Acts 16:14-15.

46 Good Characteristics Bible Drill

OBJECTIVE: Reinforces how we should live as Christians

Appropriate for age 9 to teens

When you describe somebody's fine points, you're telling what there is about him that's good. The following Bible drill Scriptures contain the names and good traits of various Bible characters. The student who first finds the Scripture should read it, tell the name of the person and what his good characteristic was.

Good Characteristics Scriptures:
1. Genesis 6:22 — Noah, obedient to God
2. Luke 10:33 — Samaritan, compassionate, showed pity
3. 2 Timothy 4:11 — Mark, helpful
4. Luke 19:8 — Zacchaeus, just or fair
5. James 5:11 — Job, patient
6. Joshua 10:25 — Joshua, courageous
7. Daniel 1:8 — Daniel, self-control
8. Luke 23:50 — Joseph, good, upright

47 Old Testament Bible Questions

OBJECTIVE: Learn and review important Old Testament facts

Appropriate for age 9 to teens

The following questions cover many of the important facts of the Old Testament. They are planned to provide variety and varying degrees of difficulty and can be used with many of the drills and quizzes in this book.

1. Who was called "the dreamer" by his brethren? Joseph — Genesis 37:17, 19
2. What did God provide for the hungry Israelites in the wilderness? Manna — Exodus 16:15.
3. With what did Adam and Eve clothe themselves when they knew they were naked? Aprons of fig leaves — Genesis 3:7.
4. In a dream, who saw a ladder reaching from earth to heaven? Jacob — Genesis 28:10, 12.
5. What great walled city fell at the sound of the trumpets and the shout of the people? Jericho — Joshua 6:1, 20.
6. What did Lot's wife become when she looked

back on the destroyed city they left? Pillar of salt — Genesis 19:26.

7. Abraham was commanded to slay his son and offer him upon an altar. What was the son's name? Isaac — Genesis 22:2.

8. With what was Job afflicted from his feet to his head? Boils — Job 2:7.

9. How many men were seen walking unharmed in the fiery furnace? Four — Daniel 3:25.

10. Naomi had two daughters-in-law. One of them was named Orpah. Who was the other? Ruth — Ruth 1:4.

11. What mother carried a little coat to her son in the temple every year? What was her son's name? Hannah, mother of Samuel — 1 Samuel 2:18, 19.

12. Who was the oldest man in the Bible? Methuselah — Genesis 5:26.

13. In what book is found both the longest and the shortest chapters of the Bible? Psalms 119 and 117.

14. In the beginning, what did God create first? The heaven and the earth — Genesis 1:1.

15. What relation was Miriam to Moses and Aaron? Sister — Exodus 15:20.

16. What was the last of the plagues brought upon Pharaoh and the Egyptians because they refused to let the Israelites go? Death of firstborn — Exodus 11:5.

17. Who put out the fleece of wool to test the will of the Lord? Gideon — Judges 6:37.

18. What was the name of Saul's son who loved and befriended David? Jonathan — 1 Samuel 18:1.

19. What did God say the serpent in the Garden of Eden was to eat all the days of its life? Dust — Genesis 3:14.

20. How did Elijah get food while he was by the brook Cherith? Ravens brought food to him — 1 Kings 17:6.

21. Who was it that killed an Egyptian and as a result was distrusted by his own people? Later he became their great leader. Moses — Exodus 2:11-15.

22. Jacob had one daughter named Dinah. How many sons did he have? Twelve — Genesis 35:22.

23. Who pursued David and sought to take his

life? Saul — 1 Samuel 23.

24. For what did Abraham send his eldest servant to the land of Mesopotamia? Wife for Isaac — Genesis 24:4.

25. For what act was Daniel thrown into the lions' den? Praying — Daniel 6.

26. What man, known as the weeping prophet, was cast into the dungeon of Malchiah? Jeremiah — Jeremiah 38:6.

27. Who was Joseph's younger brother and the only other son of Rachel? Benjamin — Genesis 45:14.

28. Of what tree were Adam and Eve forbidden to eat the fruit? Tree of the knowledge of good and evil — Genesis 2:17.

29. Who explained the meaning of the handwriting on the wall at Belshazzar's feast? Daniel — Daniel 5:17.

30. Cain was a tiller of the ground. What was his brother's occupation? Keeper of sheep — Genesis 4:2.

31. Who was the man who walked with God, and God took him, so that he never saw death? Enoch — Genesis 5:24.

32. What was the name of the only woman among the judges who ruled over Israel? Deborah — Judges 4:4.

48 New Testament Bible Questions

OBJECTIVE: Learn and review important New Testament facts

Appropriate for age 9 to teens

The following questions cover many of the important facts of the New Testament. They are planned to provide variety and varying degrees of difficulty. They can be used with many of the drills and quizzes in this book.

1. To what city was Paul traveling when he saw a great light and heard the voice of Jesus? Damascus — Acts 9:3-4.
2. What disciple was sent to the Ethiopian eunuch in the chariot? Philip — Acts 8:26, 27.
3. What is the next to the last book in the Bible? Jude.
4. What was the name of the early Christian martyr who died by stoning? Stephen — Acts 7:59.
5. Who was blinded for three days when he was converted? Saul, or Paul — Acts 9:8-9.
6. On what special day did the Holy Spirit descend upon the disciples in the form of tongues of fire? Pentecost — Acts 2:1-4.
7. In what city in Syria were the disciples first called Christians? Antioch — Acts 11:26.
8. What is the Word of God called in the Christian's armor? Sword of the Spirit — Ephesians 6:17.
9. What was Paul's occupation besides preaching the Gospel? Tent making — Acts 18:3.
10. We are told to rejoice with them that rejoice and do what with them that weep? Weep with them – Romans 12:15.
11. What is the substance of things hoped for and the evidence of things not seen? Faith — Hebrews 11:1.
12. Whom did Jesus call to repentance? Sinners — Mark 2:17.
13. What happens to a person who tries to save his life? He will lose it — Matthew 16:25.
14. What will the believer who is faithful unto death receive? A crown of life — Revelation 2:10.
15. What will happen to those that mourn? They shall be comforted — Matthew 5:4.
16. What will the pure in heart see? They shall see God — Matthew 5:8.

17. What are people who are led by the Spirit of God? They are the sons of God — Romans 8:14.
18. The preaching of the cross is what unto us which are saved? Power of God — 1 Corinthians 1:18.
19. What did the Son of Man come to seek and to save? That which was lost — Luke 19:10.
20. With the heart man believeth unto righteousness; and with the mouth confession is made unto _____ ? Salvation — Romans 10:10.
21. By _____ are we saved through _____ ? By grace and through faith — Ephesians 2:8.
22. What will happen if we are not converted and become as little children? We will not enter into the Kingdom of Heaven — Matthew 18:3.
23. What defileth a man? That which cometh out of the mouth — Matthew 15:11.
24. What is the love of money? The root of all evil — 1 Timothy 6:10.
25. What will not pass away even when heaven and earth pass away? God's Words — Mark 13:31.

49 Topical Search Scriptures

OBJECTIVE: Bible verses on several subjects help students live the Christian life

Appropriate for age 9 to teens

The following Scripture verses may be used with the Bible drills and quizzes in this book. Use them to help your students learn to live the Christian life.

Ask the students to tell how the verse relates to their lives and why they think it is in the Bible. What can they learn from it?

FAITH

Psalm 5:11	Romans 5:1
Mark 9:23	Ephesians 2:8
Jeremiah 17:7	James 2:17
Proverbs 3:5	John 14:1
Colossians 1:23	1 John 5:4
Hebrews 11:1	Habakkuk 2:4
James 1:6	2 Corinthians 5:7
Isaiah 57:13	Romans 10:9
Nahum 1:7	Psalm 115:9
Isaiah 26:3	Jude 20

PRAYER

Matthew 7:7	1 Timothy 2:8
Ephesians 6:18	Jude 20
Revelation 5:8	1 Chronicles 28:9
Proverbs 15:8	Matthew 6:6
1 Chronicles 16:11	Zechariah 13:9
Philippians 4:6	Job 22:27
Hebrews 4:16	John 15:7
Psalm 27:8	James 1:5
James 5:16	Lamentations 3:57
Romans 8:26	1 Thessalonians 5:17
Psalm 145:18	

GOD

Genesis 1:1	Ecclesiastes 7:13
Hebrews 12:9	James 1:17
1 Timothy 1:17	Acts 10:34
1 Samuel 12:22	Psalm 147:5
Hosea 1:10	John 6:46
Isaiah 5:16	Exodus 20:5
Acts 15:18	Revelation 15:3
1 Timothy 6:15	1 John 1:5
Romans 11:22	Joel 2:13
Lamentations 3:25	Romans 5:8
Hebrews 13:16	1 Corinthians 2:9

SALVATION

Romans 1:16	2 Timothy 3:15
Exodus 15:2	2 Corinthians 7:10
Isaiah 1:18	Revelation 22:17
Acts 4:12	Hebrews 4:1
Philippians 2:12	Matthew 24:13
Galatians 2:16	John 11:25
John 3:3	1 Corinthians 1:21
1 Chronicles 16:35	Acts 3:19
Psalm 3:8	John 6:47
Acts 13:26	Romans 10:9
Acts 2:38	

50 Gospel Truth Quiz

OBJECTIVE: Learn of the people, places and events of Jesus' time

Appropriate for age 9 to teens

These 26 questions summarize many of the important facts and events of the Gospels, and are of varying degrees of difficulty. They can be used with many of the drills and quizzes in this book.

1. What wicked king decreed the death of all children two years old and under in the city of Bethlehem? Herod — Matthew 2:16.
2. In what book of the Bible are found the Beatitudes from the Sermon on the Mount? Matthew — Matthew 5:1-12.
3. Who was the rich publican who climbed a sycamore tree to see Jesus? Zacchaeus — Luke 19:1-4.
4. For how much did Judas bargain to betray Jesus into the hands of the priests? Thirty pieces of silver — Matthew 26:15.
5. Who was it that said to himself, "I will arise and go to my father"? The "prodigal" son — Luke 15:18.
6. With how many loaves and fishes did Jesus feed the five thousand? Five loaves, two fishes — Matthew 14:17.
7. Who was sent as "the voice of one crying in the wilderness, Prepare ye the way of the Lord"? John the Baptist — Matthew 3:1-3.
8. Whom did Jesus call the Comforter? The Holy Spirit — John 14:16.
9. Who was the woman who anointed the feet of Jesus with precious ointment and wiped them with her hair? Mary of Bethany — John 12:3.
10. How old was Jesus when He was found in the temple conversing with the learned doctors? Twelve — Luke 2:42.
11. In what form did the Holy Spirit descend upon Jesus after His baptism? Dove — Matthew 3:16.
12. What man of Cyrene was compelled to bear the cross for Christ? Simon of Cyrene — Matthew 27:32.
13. What disciple objected to wasting the precious ointment on the feet of Jesus? Judas — John 12:4, 5.
14. How long was Jesus in the wilderness tempted of the devil? Forty days — Luke 4:2.
15. Into what animals did Jesus send the devils from the demoniac of Gadara? Swine — Mark 5:13.
16. Which of the disciples refused to believe Christ's resurrection until he saw Him? Thomas — John 20:24, 25.
17. How long was there darkness over all the land when Jesus was crucified? Three hours — Matthew 27:45.
18. What ruler of the Jews came to Jesus by night? Nicodemus — John 3:1, 2.
19. Of whom did Jesus ask three times. "Lovest thou me?" Peter — John 21:15-17.
20. In what place did Jesus pray and shed "as it were great drops of blood"? Gethsemane — Luke 22:39-44.
21. Who said to Jesus, "Lord, remember me when thou comest into Thy kingdom"? Thief on the cross — Luke 23:39-42.
22. In the parable of the lost sheep, 99 were in the fold. How many had gone astray? One — Matthew 18:12.
23. In what town did Mary and Martha live? Jesus stayed in their home often. Bethany — John 11:1.
24. Who were the two Old Testament prophets who appeared with Christ at the Transfiguration? Moses and Elias — Matthew 17:3.
25. To whom did Jesus say in the hour of His death, "Behold thy mother"? Apostle John the beloved disciple — John 19:26, 27.
26. How many lepers were healed but only one gave thanks? Ten — Luke 17:12-15.

51 | Stolen Treasures Bible Drill

OBJECTIVE: Scriptures reveal secrets about stolen treasures

Appropriate for age 9 to teens

Use these Scriptures for a Bible drill. The first student who finds each Scripture is to answer the following questions (award one point for each correct answer given): Where was the treasure? What was it? Who got it?

Stolen Treasure Bible Drill Scriptures:
1. 1 Kings 15:18 (Treasury in the Lord's temple; silver and gold; Ben-hadad)
2. 2 Kings 12:18 (Treasury in the Lord's temple; gold; king of Syria)
3. 2 Kings 14:13-14 (Temple and palace; gold and silver; king of Israel)
4. 2 Kings 16:8 (Lord's temple and treasury of palace; silver; king of Assyria)
5. 2 Kings 24:11, 13 (Lord's temple and treasury of palace; treasures and gold articles; king of Babylon)

52 Prayer & Promise Drill

OBJECTIVE: Teaches God's response to man's requests

Appropriate for age 9 to teens

This Bible drill emphasizes man's prayer requests and the promises from God in answer to such prayers.

Give the students the first reference, have them find and read the verse, and tell what the request is. Then give the second reference, have them find and read the verse, and give God's response.

These verses may also be used with other Bible quiz formats in this book, or invent another way of playing.

Man's Prayers, God's Response Scriptures:

Prayer: Psalm 63:1 — O God, Thou art my God, early will I seek Thee.

Promise: Proverbs 8:17 — Those that seek Me early shall find Me.

Prayer: Jeremiah 15:15 — O LORD . . . remember me, and visit me.

Promise: Jeremiah 29:10 — I will visit you, and perform My good word toward you.

Prayer: Psalm 143:1 — Hear my prayer, O LORD.

Promise: Isaiah 41:13 — I the LORD thy God will hold thy right hand, saying unto thee, Fear not: I will help thee.

Prayer: Genesis 24:42 — O LORD . . . prosper my way which I go.

Promise: Genesis 24:40 — The LORD . . . will send His angel . . . and prosper thy way.

Prayer: Psalm 25:4 — Shew me Thy ways, O

LORD; teach me Thy paths.

Promise: Micah 4:2 — He will teach us of His ways, and we will walk in His paths.

Prayer: Psalm 28:9 — Save thy people . . . feed them also, and lift them up for ever.

Promise: Psalm 37:3 — Trust in the LORD, and do good . . . and verily thou shalt be fed.

Prayer: Psalm 16:1 — Preserve me, O God.
Promise: Psalm 121:8 — The LORD shall preserve thy going out and thy coming in from this time forth, and even for evermore.